Goodbye

To

You

A Girlfriend's Guide to Wake You Up
Before You Go Go through Divorce

ANNETTE MARIE WESTWOOD

The Beverly Hills Eulogy
Annette Marie Westwood
thebeverlyhillseulogy@gmail.com
(323) 452-9771

Editing by Cara Highsmith, Highsmith Creative Services, www. highsmithcreative.com
Photo by Joshua K Photo
Hair by Suah at Arianna Hair Boutique
Makeup by Tammy Pham

Some names and identifying details have been changed to protect the privacy of individuals.

eBook ISBN 978-0-9984584-4-1
Print ISBN   978-0-9984584-3-4
Printed in the United States of America
First Edition 10 9 8 7 6 5 4 3 2

DEDICATION

To Ben and Max, the two most amazing boys in the world. I love you with all of my heart. I've prepared you to become good men who treat women with love, kindness, and respect. (If you ever cheat on your wife or disrespect her you will be knock, knock, knocking on Heaven's door.)

Goodbye

To

You

Contents

Introduction

The music of the 80s has been a big part of my life since high school. When I danced with my friends we turned to the 80s dance classics like Shannon, Stevie B, and Alicia. When I went through a breakup I turned to Foreigner and Styx. Later on in life I played these 80s songs to my children. Def Leppard and Guns N' Roses can make little kids really jam out. Most important, my favorite 80s songs got me through my divorce. A little "Purple Rain" and "November Rain" tossed together with a little "It's Raining Men" can be very healing.

During my unnecessary court battles I read a ton of divorce books and self-help books. I didn't leave the house except to take my kids to school, go to the book store, or buy the six bottles of wine at the grocery store it took to get the discount. I read, drank in moderation, and listened to 80s music to get through my pain. The book I wanted to find wasn't out there. I wanted a book to make me feel better about divorce, I needed to find the humor in it. So, here it is, a book that will make you laugh if you are coping with your divorce okay and just might get you to smirk if you are taking it hard.

I really am sorry you are going through this transition; I don't wish this pain on anyone. This book has a lot to offer for a person who is considering divorce, to a person divorcing, to the single girl who dreams of getting married, and the single girl who is getting married. You can skip around in this book—take what you need and leave the rest. Even the rare women who didn't come out of a divorce a bit traumatized can find useful information in here, but I do focus more on guiding the women who are having a hard time. Divorce can affect us in different ways, and the pain of it may not hit you right away. I've seen the pain hit people years later when they are really struggling and their kids are having issues.

I'm the friend everyone calls when they have a problem and need a crazy fun outlook on their situation. I'm very truthful and direct, but I find the silver lining in all situations. If you were cheated on, you know that pain hurts like you are about to die, especially if you didn't see it coming. If your husband gave you an STD from his affair, most go away in seven days, but the broken trust can last a lifetime. I know there is no humor in it now, but there will be when you find a good, honest, loving, and kind man with a bigger penis, or your ex's mistress leaves him and he's alone, or when she gets her karmic payback for betraying another woman.

If things are not working out in your marriage and you are feeling like divorce is an option, I'm going to try to help you save your marriage (that's if you aren't in a situation where you are being cheated on or emotionally or physically abused) and wake you up before you go go. In Phase 1 I'm going to give you a big reality check about what a pain in the ass divorce is and all the consequences most people don't think about before they leave their husband, or if they know their husband is not happy and may leave soon. I'm going to try to get you to work on yourself first before you leave. Yeah, I'm going to share some female tips that may be annoying that people gave me when I was going through my divorce. But, years later I realized how important they are. Also, I'm going to try to get you to be a smart Flower and try to get your husband on board without nagging or bringing up divorce. Those two things will only make things worse for you.

If, after doing the work I recommend in Phase 1, you can't save your marriage and choose to get divorced, Phase 2 will give you a Divorce 101 and offer some ways to take care of yourself while you are going through it.

INTRODUCTION

In Phase 3 I'm going to talk to you about becoming the best you that you can be so you attract the right man the next time around, or stay happily alone and grow. To me, the last chapter is the most important chapter. Nope, it won't be about you; it's about helping others who are going to get married and might be making a big mistake. Yup, I'm going to ask you to butt in a little and give them some of the statistics on the success rates of marriages, teach them everything you know about relationships, and maybe even give them this book to read before they make the biggest decision of their lives.

My main goal in this book is to make you smile and find love again—the love of your life may just be you! I will try to bring you a little laughter, whether you stay with your husband or not. I know you're a smart Flower and will make the right decision either way. And, I'm the woman to call if you need a fabulous eulogy party after your transition.

Phase 1

Should I Stay or Should I Go

So, you're trying to decide should you stay or should you go. If you stay there will be trouble; but, if you leave it might be double. Maybe one day is fine and you're happy where you are, and then the next is black and making you think you need to leave. But, I'm here to tell you, darling, that the best thing you can do to avoid a clash you don't want to experience is to stay for a while to make sure you are making the right choices about your relationship. I'm going to tell you to cool it so you don't blow something that could be saved.

Phase 1 is about taking a minute to figure out what is driving your feelings. Before you ask yourself whether you should stay or go, ask yourself, *Why am I unhappy?*, and then look at what is contributing to that unhappiness and whether you have any power over it. Don't fly right by solutions as you rush to a decision, and don't let your emotions (which we all know can change in a flash) suck you into the hell of a divorce that could be avoided. We'll start with a reality check and then we will get into some things you can try that might save your marriage so you don't have to go through unnecessary heartache.

Chapter 1

WAKE ME UP BEFORE YOU GO GO

Something's bugging you; something ain't right, and divorce may seem like the easiest solution in the moment. But, there are so many aspects of being on your own that you may not have considered. If you have been living in a bubble for a while, you need a major reality check about what is out there waiting for you. The job market, is beyond competitive, pay is low, taxes are high, and employers like to hire millennials, so if you haven't worked for a while you could be in for a really rude awakening. The cost of living is out of control for a single person, let alone for the single mom with small children. And, do you have any idea what dating is like these days? Even though the idea of dating right now might be nauseating, we are wired to crave companionship and love; so, you will find yourself pulled back into that world eventually, and it is not pretty. Buckle up because I'm about to wake you up before you go ahead and decide to leave your husband, he decides to leave you, or you both agree to end the relationship.

A lot of women don't go into divorce realistically and end up wondering what the hell they did, but this isn't going to happen to you because you aren't going to make a decision this monumental being deaf, dumb, and blind. Right? You are going to weigh out all of your options carefully and do not only what's best for you but for your children as well.

DESTINATION UNKNOWN

Do you remember those *Choose Your Own Adventure* books from back in the day? For those of you who are too young to know what I'm talking about, I will explain: The *Choose*

GOODBYE TO YOU

Your Own Adventure series was a collection of novels for kids where the reader becomes a part of the story and they get to make choices about what the main character does or what happens to them along the way that can dramatically alter the outcome. For example, Johnny is being chased down a long, dark hallway, and at the end he has to choose to climb out the window or go through the only unlocked door. Based on what you choose for Johnny, you go to pg. 6 or pg. 10 and find out what fate awaits him. Everything that happens afterward depends on the choice you make. You are under pressure to make the right choice to get him out safely, and making the wrong choice could lead him into danger.

So, now you are choosing your own adventure. Do you turn to pg. 6 and get divorced or do you go to pg. 10 and stay with your husband? Sometimes the choices you make in your life will be simple and the outcome will be clear before you even take that step. (And can we just pause for a moment and offer thanks for those no-brainer choices since life doesn't give us many of them?) More often, we make choices having some sense of where it will lead, but we don't know for sure because real life doesn't come already written out, and people don't usually follow a script for how they will act or respond to what happens to them.

*Before we proceed, I want to make it clear that the reality checks that follow are for women who are in marriages that do not involve any emotional or physical abuse or other really destructive behavior such as addiction or infidelity. This is for the women who are unhappy for reasons they may not fully understand and may be able to work things out if they have the right motivation without risking any harm to themselves or their children. If you don't have children, leaving a marriage is far less complicated, but why not try to keep the vow you made? If you do have children, you owe it to the vow you took to your husband and your children to try to save the marriage. They say that people are only as good

4

as their word, right? Keep your word if at all possible.

You are headed into a destination unknown if you've not been through divorce before. Life is so strange when you are splitting up a marriage, so here is your first reality check, pretty Flower, and I really want you to pay attention. Maybe even read this twice to make sure it sinks in.

MONEY CHANGES EVERYTHING
You may have sworn everlasting love to each other and had the belief that it was enough. But, as the saying goes, money does change everything, especially in a divorce. As a married person, you have established a certain standard of living. You may not have to worry about paying the bills, might be able to stay home with the kids, and, at the very least, have a partner to share the load (unless the whole reason you're considering kicking him to the curb is that he is gambling away your grocery money, but that falls under the list of things in my disclaimer). You need to know that, if you divorce, your standard of living is likely to decrease. You may feel like you're never gonna dance again, but you will be cleaning again if you can't afford a housekeeper. And, as messed up as it is and as strange as it might seem, his standard of living will most likely increase. This happens for several reasons:

1. Men usually earn more than women.
2. Men usually have more financial resources to fall back on.
3. Women often stay home to raise their children or only work sporadically, creating an absence from the workplace that can be a great disadvantage if they have to go back to work after a divorce.
4. Men usually don't get custody of the children and the amount of support they are ordered to pay often is not enough to realistically cover living expenses.

5

GOODBYE TO YOU

I know it may sound callous to jump right into the money issue, but it has a far-reaching effect on every other aspect of your life and if you aren't clear on what you might be facing, you could end up regretting your choices.

Now, let's get into some of the specifics of what to expect.

OUR HOUSE

Are you tired and need a rest? Is there always a crowd of people and you're trying to prevent a mess All of that stress may be making you think it's time for someone to move out, but the harsh reality of divorce is that separate households may not solve your problems, and it is sure to add more to the pile. The ways divorce affects you, your family, and even your friends are bigger than you may realize. Your house and all of your private business could end up in the middle of the street, so you need to consider the fallout I'm about to cover very carefully before you make any decisions you can't take back.

TAKE ME HOME

Your first instinct after divorce may be running home to your mom. If your marriage falls apart and you are living in a different state or country from the rest of your family, you might be saying, "Take me home!," but you need to remember that you probably won't have that option because you won't be able to move out of the state with your children unless the courts and/or your ex give you permission. If he does give you permission, you will have to pay to fly them back and forth to see him. Can you afford to do that on your salary? Are you okay with your kids flying alone? Or, alternatively, if you have to stay where you are, will you be okay seeing your extended family once per year? You may end up feeling like a prisoner for the rest of your life. Splitting up your family has big consequences and most of them are unpleasant, so consider this carefully before you make a move.

FUNKYTOWN

Yeah, you've talked about it, talked about it, and talked about it, and nothing seems to get resolved, so now you're talking about movin'. But, the move you may be facing could end up taking you straight to Funkytown. Moving is one of the greatest stressors in life, even if it's a move that is right for you. It ranks right up there along with a death, major illness, or job loss. And, guess what . . . divorce is also on that list, so you are now combining two of the most anxiety-inducing life events you can experience. I hope you get a good divorce settlement because you are going to need a lot of massages, wine, sedatives, and hair dye to deal with all the ways your body is going to respond to all of that stress.

EVERY TIME YOU GO AWAY

We all need time to ourselves to rest and regenerate so we can be the best moms ever, but when you are divorced, your kids are going to be the ones who move on a regular basis, going between your house and your ex's place. And, Flower, I can promise you, every time they go away they will take a piece of you with them. Some families have managed to have the parents alternate nights staying in the house so the kids don't have to move; but, unless you have enough money to maintain three households, this isn't a realistic option.

Either you or your ex are going to have to move after divorce. There's just no way around it, unless you have the crazy notion that you can live in the same house and not be married. What's worse is your kids are going to be continually uprooted as they go between your house and your ex's place. I know a lot of people who turn down amazing, high-paying jobs because they don't want to deal with the horror of

GOODBYE TO YOU

traveling several times per year. Packing and unpacking even for a vacation is an irritation that can take the enjoyment out of your experience. And the odds are good you will have forgotten something you need or really wanted to take with you, and that adds stress. This is what is going to happen to your children. Can you imagine being forced to move every other week for the next ten to eighteen years? That's a pretty selfish thing to ask of anyone, but especially children.

This doesn't even take into consideration the possibility that you can't afford to keep your home and will have to sell, which could mean moving your kids out of their school zone and away from their friends. They are going to give you enough normal drama as they hit puberty. Don't add this to the mix unless you absolutely have to.

18 & LIFE
Eighteen and life to go. Sounds like a prison sentence, right? You may not feel that way about your kids; but. if you end up divorced, you're going to feel that way about your ex. If you have kids together, you are tied to them for life because even when the child support runs out, there are still times when your kids will need involvement from both parents (college, weddings, grandchildren, etc.). How do you look in vertical stripes, Flower? Orange is not really the new black and never will be.

YOU SPIN ME ROUND
Being single may look like it's lots of fun, and you may want some. But, if you have kids, you and your ex are the least important people in the divorce. I will never understand counselors who tell people that kids will be just fine after their parents split up. Of course your children will survive after you traumatize the shit out of them. They don't have a choice! They can even thrive, but it takes a lot of work and a

8

firm commitment from you to help them through the healing process (and, trust me, you don't get to the place where you can do that without help for yourself). Sometimes divorce is unavoidable, and I'm totally not judging you for that. I divorced my ex twice, so, seriously, no judgment here. You must always do what is right for you! But, if you are just bored with you husband or if the problems in your marriage are fixable, do everything you can to save it because your divorce is going to affect your kids profoundly.

MISSING YOU

You can tell yourself you aren't missing them, and that it is so great being able to have the house to yourself and finally, finally get to take a bath uninterrupted, have a glass of wine, and watch something on TV that isn't animated. You can tell yourself that; but, we all know the truth, and you aren't fooling anyone. So, have you thought about how are you going to handle the custody? Will it be 50/50? Will it be the standard weekends and alternating holidays? Are you prepared for not seeing your kids whenever you want and having to miss out on some Christmases and birthdays? That's what happens when you split up and it gets really lonely and frustrating when you ship them off to the other parent, and that's even with it being on good terms. You're supposed to be with the ones you love on the significant days in their lives, and I don't think you can possibly have any idea how hard it will be on you the first time you spend a special occasion without them.

Assuming you don't have family drama like your drunk uncle who says wildly inappropriate things at Thanksgiving, the holidays are a happy time with family and friends. Well, all of that is likely to come to a screeching halt after divorce. If you get a standard visitation agreement, you're going to be alternating holidays with your ex and you're going to end up standing in front of your Christmas tree alone while your kids may be miles away, and you'll be wondering why you let them leave. It's not fun, Flower, and it is one of the brutal realities of divorce.

And, God forbid your ex has already moved on and some strange woman is the one getting to spend the holiday with your children. There is no amount of therapy or alcohol that will help you get okay with that. Now think about what it will be like to be without your child on the day you gave birth to them. Yes, your ex and his new special friend could pull right up in your driveway in his little red corvette from his midlife crises and stick your birthday boy or girl in the cramped back seat. AND, adding insult to injury, they will all get to be at your kid's party where you aren't welcome. No cake for you! You can lie to yourself and say it doesn't matter because you can celebrate on a different day, but you will be missing them in ways you can't imagine. A friend told me that it would get easier in time, but she lied to me to make me feel better; it doesn't ever get easier. You can just tolerate it better.

BACK AND FORTH

You're going to see them go back and come forth, but it won't be a dance party. It will feel like a tug-of-war. If they don't like being with your ex and beg you not to go, it will be heart-wrenching. But, let me tell you, Flower, you might be surprised to know it will be just as painful if they love going over there and it seems like they don't miss you when they are away. Remember what it was like when you dropped them off at kindergarten or daycare and they cried and didn't want you to leave, and then when you rushed back to them at the end of the day they cried because they didn't want to go home? Now imagine that, but this time they are choosing someone you don't like over you!

When you and your spouse had kids, you knew you were committing to a lifetime of love and worry. It goes with the territory; but, if you divorce, the strains of parenthood can double if you and your ex are no longer on the same page. Be sure you're ready to parent on your own and potentially face lots of opposition because that's what often comes with divorce.

WHEN THE CHILDREN CRY

If you have kids under the age of eighteen, you are going to have the worst issue in the world called *child support*. I'm going to lightly touch on this here, mainly just to give you a heads up of what you can expect. I will go into way more detail on the harsh realities of this issue in Phase 2. All you need to know now is that a lot of men believe you are just wasting their child support on getting your hair and nails done when the reality is what you get will barely help you cover living expenses and the nonstop, costly needs of your growing children. Just a little warning, if you are dealing with an angry ex, he could be willing to shell out thousands of dollars in attorney's fees just to spite you and keep you from getting a penny more than he thinks you should have. Even if your husband is a great, giving man, he may fight you on it if he didn't want the divorce. Divorce shows you who people really are! They may focus on hurting you because they are so hurt. And, if they move on quickly, they may fight you over every last penny because they only care about themselves and their new family. Remember, women still make 78 cents to the dollar a man earns. Things still aren't fair for women out there in the work force. You are most likely going to need this money for your children. You may find you and the children are crying when you can't pay the rent or can't afford to eat. If that happens, can you tell them at least you tried . . . to save the marriage?

THE WINNER TAKES IT ALL

GOODBYE TO YOU

I hate to tell you this, pretty Flower, but just because you were the bigger person in the marriage and decide you will take the high road in the divorce, there is no guarantee you are going to come out on top after your divorce. In fact, you could end up losing everything. He could win in court if you don't know how to fight for yourself and your children; and, if he does, he could take it all, and you'll be left standing small. Here is your wakeup call about the less obvious parts of your life at stake.

YOU'RE ONLY HUMAN

You are only human and you are bound to make your share of mistakes, but don't let your cute little Chihuahua get caught up in the one you're about to make. In a divorce, deciding who gets your furry friend is no different from who gets the pool table in the eyes of the law. Around 65 percent of U.S. households have a pet. If you don't have children in your marriage, your furry friend is probably like a child to you. The number of custody battles involving animals is increasing. Judges end up having to decide who gets the dog and if the other party has the right to have visitation. The courts are overwhelmed with child support/custody matters and they just don't have the time to give the same protection to animals, although animals under stress can really suffer. If you ex is vindictive, it's probably not even about the love for the animal. It can simply be about his control issues. If your ex repeatedly takes you to court, he's more concerned about controlling you and the situation than about the animal getting stressed out. These disputes can cost thousands of dollars, and the outcome can be shocking and devastating.

PEOPLE ARE PEOPLE

Everyone complains about their family—their judgmental mother, nosy sister, overbearing father—but don't let anyone else put them down. Am I right?! I hope you don't get along too awfully with your family because you are going to need them if you decide to get divorced. They might freak when you tell them you are considering divorce. Take your lumps and let your parents and extended family voice their concerns and worry about you; it's coming from a place of love and concern. This is painful news for them because they don't want to see you go through the agony of a broken family. Consider it a blessing that they care enough to want to stop you from possibly making a mistake. And, hopefully they will get past this disappointment and support you in whatever you choose.

Thankfully, my dad was there for me every step of the way. He's a great man. And my funny sister Lizzie sent me *Divorce for Dummies* to make me laugh and listened to me bitch a few times. But, my mother was not there for me and it really hurt. Some people won't get it, some may even side with your ex. I won't make unnecessary negative comments about my ex in my book since he is the father of my children (although he put me through hell), but I will say my mom stuck up for a man who deeply hurt me over and over again because he had a lot of money and more to offer her. That's a pain you really don't want to experience. Ultimately, it's your decision and you are the one who is going to have to live with the consequences. But, you are going to need a support system once you are on your own, so find the people who love you whether or not they agree with your decision because you will need them to get through this . . . and the rest can lovingly go to hell.

BELIEVE IT OR NOT
Well, here you are; look at you, thinking of heading into a divorce and you probably can't even believe it yourself. Get ready because here's something else you may not believe: it's not just the assets and the kids you have to split up; someone

is going to get most of the friends in the divorce, and it might not be you. Some mutual friends will act weird because they don't know what to think or who to believe about what went wrong. It could be that you have some really shitty friends and it doesn't matter who did what; it only matters who has the most influence, the most money, and the most to offer them as a friend. A divorce really is the best way to find out who your good friends are. And, here's another factor you may not have considered: You're single now and odds are good that your married female friends aren't going to be all that excited about you being around their husbands. Some women will feel threatened by your singleness, especially if their husband has already had an affair. I can't tell you how many divorced women get hit on by their friend's husbands, and then they are treated like the bad guy while the husband suffers no consequences. If you are very attractive and fit, you are in for some real single discrimination.

9 TO 5

Well, we've already talked about the reality of finances after divorce, but are you ready for doing the 9-to-5 grind and barely making a living? If you find yourself having to re-enter the workforce, there are a number of resources out there to help. The Federal Labor Department publishes Labor Statistics that will help you find the jobs with the best growth outlook so you can identify a field to explore if you've been staying at home with the kids or only working part-time. Hopefully, you already have a good job or were smart enough to go back to school before you started considering a divorce, but even so, you may find you have to put in more hours to cover increased living expenses or you may find the demands of your job are a lot harder when you don't have a partner at home to help pick up the kids or start dinner if you're working late. You have to be realistic about what your income is going to look like and if you can manage a household on it alone because you can't count on child and spousal support to cover everything if you get it. Here's your reality check on what it's going to look like going back into the workforce if you've been out of it for a while.

EVERYBODY WANTS TO RULE THE WORLD

Are you ready to take on the world and conquer it? I hate to burst your bubble, but the world kept going and changing while you were at home with the kids, and they don't care that you were the best PTA president the school had ever seen. That does not translate into real-world corporate experience. We've covered the logistics and emotional upheaval of leaving kids, managing schedules, and figuring out finances; but, if you have not been in the work force for a while, you have another rude awakening. While you might be awesome at making creative, healthy snacks that your kids love or be a master at getting glitter off of all the surfaces it can cling to, those skills won't make for an impressive resume.

Think I'm being condescending and dismissive by saying that's all you have to offer after staying at home with your kids? Well, get ready, because that's exactly how a hiring manager is going to make you feel. Even if you have an impressive degree from an Ivy League school, if you haven't used it in ten years and haven't kept up with the changes in your field, it's going to be nearly useless. I'm not saying you won't be able to find a job, just that you could be facing an uphill battle. You may have to settle for a job you feel is beneath you, struggle to learn new things, and feel out of place with all of the Kimberlys and Tristans who have nothing but time to focus on making you feel inferior because your experience is so outdated. I know it sounds harsh, but this is part of your reality check to help you understand what lies ahead so you can weigh your options with all the knowledge you can possibly have ahead of time.

GOODBYE TO YOU

IF YOU LEAVE

It's a classic scene: eyes red from a flood of tears, snot streaked from cheek to cheek, choking sobs of misery . . . and that's just you sitting in the car after you pried your kid off of your ankle so you could rush off to work. If you leave your children who are used to being home with you, dropping them at daycare could turn into a daily struggle of them refusing to let go at any price. My kids cried and cried, and I cried all the way to work for almost a year. Who wants to start each day with that kind of torture? If your kids are older, they may have to ride the bus home and return to an empty house. Ever heard the term "latchkey kid"? Those are the ones whose parents work long hours and who have to fend for themselves after school, sometimes for several hours. If you don't want your child to be alone, then you'll be putting them in an aftercare program, which costs money you probably don't have. Then you'll be racing against the clock to pick them up before closing and heading to a drive-thru because it's already dinner time (or past) and you're just too beat to cook anything when you get home. And, that is neither a healthy nor economical way to feed your family. For some families, this is already part of life, and their kids are already used to this; but if you've been at home and available to them, this new reality for your children is going to be a harsh adjustment. Heartbreaking won't be a strong enough word to describe how you'll feel. Just keep that in mind as you plan to divorce.

FIGHT FOR YOUR RIGHT

You wake up late for school and the kids don't want to go. Or they could be sick or school is closed for a teacher in-service day or there's a school field trip your kids have begged you to chaperone. These demands on your time that were much easier when your husband was around (even if he didn't participate in them) now require taking time off work, which

16

eats up your paid time off. Suddenly your vacation is no longer a trip to the beach or a theme park; it's a trip to the doctor or a meeting with the principal. Sounds fun, right? Obviously, we are going to put our kids first, and do the best we can for them, but divorce can make that harder than it has to be. It introduces challenges you never would imagine, unless you happen to have a friend already going solo who shares her tales of woe. Even then, you won't fully grasp the compromises you'll face and the disappointments you'll have to manage until you are in it. I've never missed a school performance that my children participated in. The look of joy on their faces when they saw me snapping pictures or with tears in my eyes because I was so proud of them was something I was not going to miss. I always tried to go and take a pic of a friend's kid that had to work and make them feel special. You could see the sadness in their eyes. I couldn't even imagine how their mom felt not being able to make it to the show.

MENTAL HEALTH

Dealing with your ex throughout a divorce is going to make you want to bang your head against a wall. But, not so fast! If you don't have good insurance through your job, giving yourself a concussion is not going to help your already frustrating situation. The cost of insurance is going to drive you mad, and maybe broke if you don't have good coverage. If you are fortunate enough to have a husband with good insurance, he will have to retain coverage for the children or reimburse you for the cost of getting coverage for them. (Of course, that's no guarantee he will, especially if he's not keeping up with the base child support.) But, he does not have to keep you on his insurance, so you'll be scrambling to get some of your own. Maybe you didn't think of this little problem that will cost you about $500 per month not including dental (I hope you don't need a root canal) if you don't have a job that offers medical or haven't had a job up to this point. If you were previously covered on your husband's policy, you can continue your coverage under COBRA for up to 36 months if he works for a large company, but it will probably be double the cost to you. It is possible to include in the terms of your divorce that he has to keep you on his health insurance; but, this can become a big issue if he doesn't want to help you out in this area, and he probably already has someone else he wants to put on his plan. The perks of marriage aren't just about having someone to share your life with—the joys and the burdens. There are some very real, very expensive things that come with spousal benefits that go away when you divorce, so plan accordingly.

LOVE STINKS
Seriously, love really does stink sometimes. You love him, he loves her, and she loves somebody else, and no one is happy. But, sometimes he doesn't love you anymore and ends up with another woman, and if you think his not loving you anymore stinks, well this is going to suck really hard. It's not just about seeing your ex in the arms of another. There are very real ways they become a part of your life that can be really ugly or surprisingly tolerable, depending on what they are like.

COLORS
You could end up dealing with a nightmare walking or a psychopath talking like Pam has to endure. She had to deal with a "Colors" situation. Don't know what I mean? Stick with me and I'll explain. I'm going to spend a little more time here because I've been hearing so many terrible stories like this lately. I really want you to get this reality check about how some woman can behave when they are insecure and feel threatened. Also, I encourage you to listen to the song

"Colors" before you read this so you get the picture. I'm not kidding, go listen to what Ice-T has to say.

Pam was a stay-at-home mom of two little boys. She always put her boys first and did everything for them. Her husband was a successful executive, making a lot of money, but was not really attentive as a father or a partner and liked to drink. She had the picture-perfect life, but behind the façade things were a mess.

When she finally kicked her husband out, he put her through the court battle from hell. Being cray-cray (my term for a narcissist, since I'm not licensed to diagnose) he was rather upset because nobody got away with kicking him out for any reason, but especially not for something like drinking too much or having sexual relations with whomever he wanted. How dare she think she deserved to be treated well? He starting dating a woman from work who was a mean, ugly woman, had a lot of tacky tattoos. I will refer to her as Colors because she really is a walking nightmare. To make matters worse, her ex also started dating her best friend who looked like Heather Locklear.

When her kids would return from weekend visitations with him, they reported that Colors played with them during the day; and, when she left, her Heather Locklear-looking now ex-friend slept over. Can you imagine her horror? They weren't even divorced yet, only separated, and he was playing house (in Pam's house) with both girlfriends!

Somewhere in this mess, Pam's ex-friend went back to her former boyfriend, so Colors won her ex by default. Colors inserted herself in their divorce, making false statements about Pam and creating additional conflict while the settlement process was underway.

She moved right into Pam's home as soon as she got the opportunity, which shows what poor judgment she has. Please really pay attention here for a minute: your ex's new girlfriend can move into the home that you own if you move out, and there is nothing you can really do about it. Most women have too much class to move into your home, but some women have no shame. If a woman pulls a move like this, she should at least have to get your permission and work out a rent payment with you for living in the home that you own. Maybe you're the rare woman who wouldn't care if a woman was freeloading in the house that you own, and that's fine; but, think of it this way: if your house is for sale due to your divorce and her poor taste extends to decorating, you could have trouble selling the home and lose money.

So, when Pam met this new woman for the first time, Colors grabbed her arm and yelled terrible things in front of her children and threw a bottle at her. Her younger son got so upset that he vomited, and her older son started to cry. To make matters worse, she wrote a statement for the court that Pam was the one who did those things to her. The statement Colors wrote went and on about what a terrible person she was though she didn't know her at all—only what her boyfriend told her.

The worst part of her court statement was that she blamed Pam for a medical issue her son was having. It was bad enough her son was dealing with this issue, but now it was announced to the world in court papers. I don't know how someone could do that to a child! I don't know how Pam's ex let her do that to his child! She claimed to care about her boyfriend's children, yet she was willing to embarrass one of them publicly to punish his mother. She also said many other ridiculous things that are better left unsaid. But I do need to share this one thing because I laughed my ass off when I heard about it. (I always look for humor in difficult situations to help deal with them better.) Colors wrote in a court document that her boyfriend (Pam's ex) was cheating on her with his soon-to-be-ex-wife's best friend, and that Pam was happy about it.

Colors had basically just helped show the court that

Pam's soon-to-be-ex was a real piece of work! I know, it doesn't even make sense why she would ever admit that in a court document! This shows how crazy some women can be. As if dating a guy going through a divorce wasn't enough, he was cheating on her with his wife's friend. And all of that on top of the fact that both of these women were mistresses he had while still married. What do you even say to that? Colors, Colors, Colors, Colors . . .

I get so perplexed by women who stick up for men they barely know and will even try to destroy another woman's life for a man who hasn't even given them a real commitment. I understand that most women would never do something like this, only someone with severe psychological issues, but this stuff happens in divorce more than you may want to think about. If your ex has issues, he will attract someone with issues, and you will have two people with issues beating you up in court, maybe for the rest of your life if you have kids together. The court is usually smart and knows it's a jealousy issue and those statements are lies, but this stuff happens every day and you should be aware before you get divorced. If you want to leave your husband because he's cray-cray, just know the cray-cray can get worse.

I feel the need to give you a little more of this story for a full reality check of what the cards may deal you for your future life. Eventually, her ex married Colors. She did all the things that her husband should've been doing for the kids—she called the school, handled their medical issues, and even wrote out the children's child support check though she wasn't authorized on his bank accounts. She stuck her nose in wherever she could to hurt Pam and control her husband. Her behavior was vindictive and petty. But, my compassionate side wonders, *Who hurt her? Why does she feel so insecure, and threatened and feel the need to hurt another woman?* If we peeled back all the layers of the onion, at the core is probably a hurt, scared little girl who has some serious issues that really need to be addressed.

But be warned a woman like Colors may be taking care of your children if you chose to get divorced, and there is nothing you can do about it but drink wine, pray, and know that her karma will get her.

I'm now going to give you the flip side and tell you about an amazing woman who could marry your ex. I'm going to keep this short and simple, but know this situation is pretty rare. I gave you extremes, your husband's new wife will probably fall somewhere in the middle.

SISTER CHRISTIAN

Yes, the time has come and your ex's new wife realizes she's not the only one. She understands she is the second wife, and a first wife came before her. She has married a really nice, loving divorced man with two older daughters. Her husband had a strained relationship with his ex because she was the one who wanted the divorce. She turned his life upside down, but he tried to be amicable for the sake of the kids. He always did the right thing for them in spite of the conflict.

This second wife is a really kind person and has made an effort to become friends with her new husband's ex-wife and has treated her with respect. She tried to honor the ex-wife when she spent time with her step-daughters because it simply was the right thing to do. It was a challenge at times because this woman wasn't someone she would have chosen as a friend under normal circumstances. They were complete opposites and had nothing in common. But, by befriending his ex and being kind, the woman opened up to Sister Christian, told her what boundaries she had so they could be on great terms for the sake of everyone, and Sister Christian respected them.

She was clear about her ranking on the "mom scale;" she was number two, and she was just fine with that. She understood that in signing up to be the second wife and the stepmother, that was her place. She understood his financial obligations to his first wife and respected that too. Even though she had to work a lot and was tired all the time, she understood that was part of choosing this life with him.

The person your ex moves on with doesn't have to be a nightmare situation, though you really have no say in it. The only thing you can do is choose to be respectful, establish boundaries that honor everyone's place in the family dynamic, and, above all, keep the well-being of the kids as your primary concern.

I know, I know, I'm bring up his new wife when you are still married to the bastard, but if you do end up divorcing your husband, he most likely will get married again and soon— men don't like to be alone. Hopefully he will marry a sweet classy lady like Sister Christian. But, just remember, you could end up with a Colors situation. It's a *shot in the dark*. This horror of his new wife can last the rest of your life, or until your ex becomes a man and takes his penis back, or divorces her.

EVERY ROSE HAS ITS THORN

After your divorce you may be singing a sad, sad song for a while, but you may decide to get married again. If you do, it may seem like this new man is the rose your garden has been waiting for. Just remember that every rose has a thorn. He might come with emotional baggage from his divorce that affects your relationship. It might be that the thorn is that you end up being the second wife. Are you prepared to be a step-parent to another woman's child/children? Marriages really only work when the couple's relationship is the foundation and they come first in each other's lives. If you both put your children first, or you have a contentious relationship with them, how is this going to work out for you?

Getting into a second marriage may present more problems than you have now! I was my ex-husband's second wife and he was my first husband. He didn't have kids with his first wife, but he gave her a lot of alimony. I'll admit I was upset that he was giving her a lot of money because he told me she cheated on him, and I took him at his word. We were young and having a tough time starting our life together because of the amount of money he had to give her. I knew my place as second wife and that comes with the territory, but I don't think money should be given to people who break the marital contract. She took a vow to be with him for life and she broke it. Why would she get his money? Plus, they didn't have children and she was living with another man! But, in time, he admitted he cheated on her too. So, I don't know who the hell should've been given what since they both broke the marital contract. I just know I felt really bad that I believed his lies. Point being, understand that you will never know all sides of a relationship story and get clear on if you can handle being a second wife or not.

I really love children and wish I'd had more, but I know I wouldn't be able to deal with all the complications that come with being a step-mother. You have to really know yourself and what works for you and stick with it. Don't kid yourself into thinking you can handle being with a man with child support, custody, and alimony responsibilities if you are expecting to have a simple life with no external forces testing your relationship. You will be called upon to put up with a lot of less than ideal aspects of your relationship and home life. Think about all the ways your ex's new life affects you and then remember there is another woman feeling the same about you. If you think you're not cut out for it, don't date men with children. I know a lot of women who won't date men with children because they want a simple life. Marriage is hard enough without the extra complications. Don't set yourself up to fail in a marriage that's not going to work for you.

SITUATION

It's very easy to judge another person's situation from the outside looking in, but there is a 99.99% chance you are going to be wrong, so be careful as you form opinions about what someone else is experiencing in their relationship or the ending of it. You only have part of the information after all.

A while back I attended a lovely dinner with six amazing women and we were discussing our ex-husbands' vocations and custody issues we faced. One woman who was having some first wife issues said this to me when she found out my ex was successful: "You're so lucky that you get a lot of money." I don't think she realized just how insulting and stupid that sounded. I am not lucky because I am getting any amount of financial support. I would much rather have kept my family together instead of being given a check to raise our children alone and dump them in daycare while I worked (since I wasn't really getting the kind of money she imagined I was). I even remarried my ex because I wanted to try to salvage things to give my kids a happy home and grow old with their dad. I personally wouldn't have had children if I'd known I would have to work full-time. I know my limitations; I'm not a superwoman and can't do it all. I never wanted to be divorced, and now I get support checks because my dream and my family were shattered . . . *but she thinks I'm lucky?* Maybe, she values money more than family and love, but I certainly don't. I was livid. My life was turned upside down and my heart was broken, but I'm lucky that I get checks that give me money to take care of my kids all alone. Fuck-to-the-You! Women love being loved and most women will tell you they wanted a husband and children from the time they were little girls. Who would rather get a check than be with a loving man and their family at Christmas?

I know it makes some second wives feel better to see the first wives as lazy and greedy for trying to get child support, but it is usually to overcompensate for being called gold diggers. As a second wife, you can't trust your new husband's account of what made the marriage fall apart, so don't judge the first wife based on what he tells you. And to the first wives, I would remind you that part of your judgment of the second wife is coming from the pain of loss and fear that you and your kids won't have what you need and fear of her pretending to be mom to your children. Give each other a chance and try to make the new family configuration work. First wives deserve what has been awarded to them by the court, especially if there are kids involved. She may have given up a career to take care of her family and trying to re-enter the workforce is not as easy as it is for someone fresh out of college. And, unless the second wife was the mistress, they aren't the source of the problems that broke up the marriage. This first wife, second wife, third wife judgement needs to stop! In time most women find out why the ex left or what BS she had to deal with. Again, none of us are perfect, and I guarantee you will never know the entire true saga of what happened in the relationship. But, for the sake of the kids, you should try to give the benefit of the doubt and never do anything to hurt each other. We need to figure out a bro code like what the guys have!

DON'T GET ME WRONG

You may find love again later on if you chose to get divorced, but second (or third or fourth, etc.) marriages have lots of challenges of their own. Please don't get me wrong, many second marriages turn out amazing, especially if you marry later on in life when your children are on their own and the relationship focus can be you and your new love. You could find the love of your life with the guy who was born to be your man and live happily ever after like a fairytale. If you are fortunate enough to experience that, all the pain you went through in marrying too young when you didn't know how difficult marriage was or what to look for in a partner will no longer exist because you've found a good man that makes your heart smile.

But, the only way to make sure that is the case is to learn from your past mistakes and go into your next relationship with your eyes open to the delicate balance of give and take and the unique challenges that come from blending families or starting over with someone after having your heart broken. My point is this: all relationships require work. Don't be fooled into thinking that if it's meant to be you won't have any challenges. People are complicated and they bring all of those complications into relationships. The only way to deal with them is to understand that being "made for each other" is just the start.

HOLD ME NOW

He said he has a picture pinned to his wall? In 2018 that means, he has a picture on his online dating profile. You may not be able to imagine it right now, but there will come a time when you'll want to get back out "there" and find someone to hold you now so the loving can start again. Let me tell you, Flower, the dating world has changed dramatically. If it's been awhile, you are in for a rude awakening. Men may give you their number, but it could be fake or it could be written on every wall from here to Timbuktu! Please, be super careful if you chose to go online. Online is how dating is done nowadays and 80 percent of people lie about their age, weight, and height. Also, beware that 10 percent of all dating profiles are fake. In 2011, there were around 5,600 online dating scams reported to the FBI. And that can't even begin to give you any numbers on the number of lies a man will tell you to get you to have sex with them as soon as possible.

I'm going to scare ya a bit here while we are talking about dating, but, while it's not a good idea to stay with your husband for fear of not finding love again, you need to be

27

aware when you leave that you don't know what the cards of life hold for you for future relationships. I have friends who have moved on to find the real hero of their lives after a divorce, but I also have friends who have yet to find anyone they would ever consider marrying as well as friends who settled and call me bitching all the time. So, let's get into your dating reality check so you have a better understanding of the hell you may face trying to date again.

DON'T YOU WANT ME

If you don't have children, you are very lucky when it comes to dating after a divorce, but if you do have children, you're not going to like this one, but this is the truth. If you are a single mother trying to date, you will find yourself asking, "Why don't you want me, baby?" more often than you can bear. The reality is there is absolutely no benefit for men to date a single mom. There are so many women out there who don't have children, have amazing jobs, and tons of free time to devote to him. Sometimes, there are troubling reasons below the surface for why those women are still single; but, sometimes the reason is simple: they were just smart enough to wait to find the right guy and know their worth. These women have a huge advantage over the women who devoted their younger years to a husband and kids and are just now back in the game.

Think about this: most women will take care of your kids, especially if they have kids of their own. Women are usually not the ones who take the most financial responsibility for children and we are natural nurtures. Why would another man want to take on the responsibility of another man's children?

Here are the reasons men don't want to date a single mom, many of which are entirely legitimate and it's hard to fault them for it:

1. ATTENTION: Unfortunately, most men are like kids themselves, and they need to come first in your life. A good single mom would refuse to put any man before her kids. And single moms end up being the mom and the dad in a lot of situations.

2. FINANCIAL REASONS: Men don't want to pay for another man's children! Men work hard for their money and spending it on children they didn't create when the man who did is failing requires a level of commitment that is hard to come by. Plus, they may have their own children they're already having to support.

3. BODY: Yes, men love a tight, toned body. All of us who have been through childbirth know that our bodies aren't what they used to be. There are men who prefer the differences of a mature woman's body; but, let's be realistic, more of them want the idealized images they see in the movies and have convinced themselves that is real and attainable.

4. THE EX: Pissing contests, cock fights, ego clashes— things get ugly when men get territorial. Your relationship may be long dead and buried, but as soon as another man comes into your life, count on your ex inserting himself and spraying everything in your world with his scent again like a feral cat. No guy wants to deal with an ex who can't respect boundaries, and no man, regardless of how much he's moved on can stand seeing another man have access to the things that used to bear his name.

COME GO WITH ME

He's only going to go with ya if you have a lot going on! This is probably what you are thinking right about now as you are contemplating getting back into dating. The website "Brain

Measures" has a calculator that uses statistical information from the US Census such as your age, education, household income, and combines it with other well-researched information such as your fitness level, whether you dated someone in the last year, and if you have the confidence to get married, and has put together a chart to predict the likelihood of getting married after a certain age. A lot of women when they reach thirty years old without having been married get scared that they are never going to meet someone. But, what happens after 40 or after 50?[1]

Age	Women	Men
30	81	84
35	66	69
40	38	41
45	33	36
50	20	23

You seriously might not meet another man. This isn't meant to scare you, and right now you might be saying, *I don't give a shit if I meet another man or not*, but as you get older and the trauma of all this is behind you, you will want to love again. Remember, you were lucky and got to experience marriage; some women have never had the chance to experience love, let alone marriage, and when you reach 50 you have a 20 percent chance of getting married—and that's if you're smart and fit, otherwise your chances are even lower.

You obviously don't stay with your husband out of fear of not finding another, but you do need to consider that life doesn't guarantee that you will meet someone amazing and fall in love again.

HERE COMES YOUR MAN

1   https://www.brainmeasures.com

Is your man really coming this way? Getting back the love you've let fade with your husband is not an easy thing. But, finding love with someone new isn't either. If you don't have a lot of friends who know single people or have a super active social life that brings you into new social circles, you're probably going to end up having to look online. That's assuming you have any free time and energy for dating after working, taking care of kids, and keeping up a household. Another thing to think about is dating travel time, this may not seem relevant, but there is a joke where I live in LA that if you live on the other side of the 405 freeway from the guy you're interested in, then you're not datable. Even five miles away, you're looking at an hour drive because of the volume of traffic and the hills and mountains that prevent you from having direct routes. We don't even have bad weather! If it's raining, most people would cancel the date where I live, let alone have to drive in snow to go on a date.

The point is there are going to be lots of obstacles to finding your man, so think carefully before you discard the one you've got.

I WANT YOUR SEX
There are things in life that you can guess, and some things you just know. But you may not know this! I don't know what you sex life is right now with your future ex-husband, but since you're thinking about getting divorced, I'm going to assume it's not going so well. Here's the reality to your future sex life. You could meet someone amazing who rocks your world; but, if you're getting older, are used to sex without condoms, or are used to a big penis, you may not want some sex or love.

MAN SIZE LOVE
Yes, we're going to talk about what you think we're going

to talk about here. The truth is you are likely to face a very harsh reality in this department. Sometimes in life you have to settle for things that could really dampen your spirit and this may be one of them. If your ex had a big penis, you are spoiled and have to come to terms with the fact that you may not get a big penis again! And that could affect the rest of your life. If you fell in love with a man with a big penis, and got used to big penis sex and now you have to have average or small penis sex you may feel really disappointed. I know this isn't the be-all-end-all of traits you need in a man, but it is an important factor that can affect how you feel about anyone new. No matter what we tell our men, size (whether length or girth) does matter. Sure, whether he knows what to do with it or not matters almost as much, but let's be real . . . size is still the deciding factor. Being able to manage money well doesn't matter if you don't have any to manage. Get what I'm saying?

According to my research, the average length of an erect penis is 5.16 inches and 4.69 inches for the girth. Sit down now and don't sip your wine while you're reading this; you could choke and I don't want to be responsible. Out of 100 men, only five would have a penis longer than 6.3 inches. According to most studies, women want a man who has a man-size love tool around 6.3 inches and the girth was an important factor as well. So, if you had/have a man with a big penis, you have a very low chance of getting that again. If you're on the fence about getting the divorce, this one factor may be big enough to tip the scale in the right direction. But, who knows, maybe your ex had a small/average penis and you'll get an upgrade! As we move on to the next issue, take another a big sip of wine, or refill your glass.

SOLID

As men get older some things are just not solid as a rock anymore. What if your new man can't perform without some intervention . . . or a lot of intervention! Imagine your disappointment when you've been looking forward to intimacy again and the response is non-existent. And the older you get, the more likely you are to date men with this issue. This is one of the reasons my friends are dating younger men. They are in their prime sexually and don't want to deal with issues or disappointment after a divorce. Sex is really important in a relationship and when you were in a loveless and/or sexless marriage this issue can truly be awful. But, maybe this is your reality now, and you will find a good man who is solid as a rock, and build it up, and up, and up. Yup, one more thing to think about.

CAN'T FAKE THE FEELING

Seriously, I want you to think long and hard about the fact that you really can't fake that feeling in your body. If you start dating, you will have to wear condoms. If you're not used to condom sex, it could be awful. Everyone knows sex with condoms doesn't feel as good. Even if you date someone for a long time, I don't recommend the condom coming off until you are engaged. A lot of men carry HPV, and it's serious. You could get cervical cancer. If he's been single for a while and slept with one or two woman he probably has it, and you don't because you've been married for a long time. You can't risk taking any chances until you have a solid commitment. I know, I know, maybe you're still married and think this reality check is crazy; but, when that small, limp penis wrapped in plastic comes at you, you will remember what I just told you.

HARD HABIT TO BREAK

Not a single person I've spoken with about their divorce thought it would be as hard as it was. Even if they really wanted the divorce, it can be a hard habit to break, they thought they would be here forever! They thought things wouldn't be as complicated as they turned out. Endings do bring new beginnings, but new beginnings always come with an ending, and most of the time those endings are painful on some level.

Let me tell you, you can be a really strong woman who can handle a lot; but, if you think you will get through this unscathed, think again. You can't love someone and not feel the pain of loss when that relationship comes to an end. You may be rid of your old problems, but new problems are on the way, because that's life.

I hope this chapter has let you see a little of what really is on the other side of the fence so you can make a carefully considered decision about divorce instead of just rushing into it thinking it is a quick fix.

If *nothing is gonna stop us now* from going to file divorce, let's move along. But, if I've caused you to stop for a minute and reconsider, good. That was my goal. Now let's move on to things you can do to potentially avoid divorce and improve your marriage.

Chapter 2
SHE'S GOT THE LOOK

Are you tasty like a raindrop and got the look? Yeah, I don't think I know anyone who is tasty like a raindrop (and I'm not sure I'd even consider a raindrop tasty), but I know a lot of women who've got the look. They look like butter most of the time, they have a strong sense of self, and they put their own happiness first. They haven't forgotten the things they enjoyed about life and have made room for them as their lives expanded to include husbands and children. I think women are taught that this is selfish, but it's not at all; it's essential if you want to be the best you for those you love and who depend on you. What have you got going on pretty, Flower?

I'm sure you're thinking, *But, my husband is the one who should change; plus, he's a real dick most of the time! He's the one who should be working to fix this. Why should I always be the one?* I get it, but it could save your marriage and save you a lot of future pain if you look at your fabulous self in the mirror and consider what you can work on as well. And don't tell me there's nothing; none of us are flawless, as much as we like to throw that word around. I'm not asking you to turn your brown eyes blue. I'm asking you to take notice of where personal growth and beauty can be developed more. Seriously, if anything that I suggest that pisses you off then that's where you start. When something hits a nerve, that's a pretty good clue it's a place where growth is needed.

HOT HOT HOT
Are *you* feeling hot, hot, hot? If not, chances are your husband may be struggling to feel that way about you too. Please don't think out loud, "Fuck You, Annette," in this section. I get it; I thought the same thing about people who talked about

looking good in relationships books when I could barely function because I was upset. It's not easy when you feel this kind of pain so you just don't care anymore and have given up. If that's where you are in this transition, I'll give you space to be sad; but, at least brush your pretty hair and put on a nice bathrobe. But, the thing is, how you feel about yourself definitely translates into what you put out there and affects the way others perceive you. I didn't make the rule; it just is what it is.

I was talking to one of my gay friends and he brought up the fact that he never understood why some women let themselves go in marriage. His straight male friends would complain that their wife gained weight and didn't put as much effort into her appearance as she did when they were dating. He also noticed his straight female friends let themselves go a bit after they got married. He said in the gay world they look better and try harder when they have a boyfriend because they want their boyfriends to think they are hot and not leave them. All of that made me think they are onto something. I looked around at my married friends and some did gain weight and many had stopped doing the fun things they did before they got married. So, here is where I'm going with this . . . let's get you back to the way you looked before you were married as best we can so you can feel good about yourself. Yes, men are visually-oriented creatures, and it's important for him to think you are sexy, but he is just the bonus beneficiary of this effort. You need to feel great about you for you. Plus, if you do leave him, you will have to look Hot, Hot, Hot if you want to find love again. And, since you may have to do this anyway in your future, why not start now and jump ahead of the game. If you save your marriage, great, if you don't, you look like butter and will attract a new man to divorce someday! I'm not sure if I'm kidding or not! Anywho, you deserve to feel you are at your best all the time.

So, where do you start? Maybe you've lost yourself

so much that you don't even remember what kinds of things made you happy. Let me give you some ideas.

PUTTING ON THE RITZ

If you're blue and you don't know where to go, start with getting out of your rut and change things up a bit. "Puttin' on the Ritz" means dressing very fashionably—getting all dolled up—and that's exactly what you need to do while you're in transition. I understand it might not be realistic for the everyday stuff, but even a little extra effort like putting on a little makeup or wearing jeans and a nice shirt instead of yoga pants and a hoodie to the store will make a big difference in how you feel as you walk out of the house.

When you get up in the morning, dress well and look as good as you can. Do this so you feel good about yourself and the beautiful day ahead of you. If you haven't heard the song "Puttin' on the Ritz" in a while, play it loud and go dig through your closet to find something you haven't worn in ages. Have fun and treat yourself to a little personal fashion show or imagine you're going to a spectacular red carpet event. It will lift your spirits and you'll find yourself wanting to do a little extra all the time. I'm not saying be "Extra" where everything is over the top. And, if you already make this effort, maybe it's a matter of a subtle change in your style to get you feeling fresh and vibrant again. Just try something different so you can see yourself in a new light. You'll thank me for it, Flower.

MY ADIDAS

Are your shoes funky fresh? Do they give you a little swagger in your step? If not, then go out and get a new pair of shoes! If you are over forty and don't have at least one pair of fabulous high black heels, close my book and get your tuchus to the store! I don't care how tall you are; you must have a great pair of heels because they make any shape of legs look sexy. You never need to pay full price; there are plenty of discount stores that have clearance stock of great shoes that won't ever go out of style.

LOOKS THAT KILL

She's got the looks that kill and it starts at the top of her head. There is a saying that a woman's hair is her crowning glory, and it's true! Have you ever watched those wedding dress shopping shows where the woman tries on these beautiful gowns and her hair is in a ponytail? It kills the whole look. The dress doesn't shine nearly as brightly and she looks a little out of place in it. Do you know why? Because her hair isn't done to match the rest of her.

You don't have to have a bridal "do" every day of the week, but spending a little extra time to give it some style will keep you from looking like you just rolled out of the bed to show up to your life. Also, if you are finding yourself frustrated every morning when getting ready, you might need to change things up a bit or have some shape put back into your hair after it's grown. Having some fun with your hair can make you feel really good about yourself.

Let's be real; as women, we all like when people tell us how pretty we look. It's not just men who take notice when we look good; women notice us as well. When I see a pretty girl, I want to go right up to her and tell her how pretty she is and want to know what she's wearing and what makeup and moisturizer she uses, maybe even the name of her plastic surgeon and dermatologist (work with me here, I live near Beverly Hills).

So, go get a new haircut and maybe try some highlights or just punch up your natural color a little. You'll be amazed at how even a subtle change like that can make you feel alive in a new way.

FRESH

One of the most successful marketing tools is a fresh-faced woman. She looks vibrant and happy and carefree. The reality is, the first thing people notice is your face. If you have smooth glowing skin, people are drawn to you. They want to know your secret and they don't always realize it's your bright skin they are drawn to.

Of course, in our cynicism, when an older woman looks young we all assume we know her secret: Botox or plastic surgery. There are also injectable fillers to plump up sagging skin like Juvederm® and Restylane®. But not everyone resorts to such drastic measures. Sometimes a quality facial, chemical peel, or age spot remover from a dermatologist can bring back your youthful glow. A Clairsonic® skin brush is also a great, much cheaper option. It's my favorite beauty product. But, if you just have a good skincare regimen from the beginning it will help you avoid the need for a lot of these other treatments. Making sure you clean and hydrate your skin well (from the outside *and* the inside) is the best way to take care of yourself for long-lasting results.

Another really easy way to have a big impact on how bright and youthful your face looks is having pretty, white teeth. This one detail can boost your confidence and make you more comfortable smiling, which makes you look younger and happier. I highly recommend you invest in a whitening tray from your dentist or some Crest White Strips®, especially if you drink coffee, tea, red wine, or anything else that stains. Yellow teeth make you look older than you are.

Here's one last tip for accentuating your facial features to draw the right kind of attention: eyelash extensions. If you haven't tried these, please just do it once. You don't even need to wear makeup when you get eyelash extensions. It's insane how well they work to make your eyes more dramatic and bright. There is a downside: it does take a long time to have them professionally applied and they don't last a long time.

But, while you have them on you seriously feel like butter!

LIES

Lies, lies, lies. Is plastic surgery deceptive on a certain level? It's been criticized for a long time as cheating, but it has become more acceptable in the last decade. Do you wear makeup? Because that's deceptive. Do you have a padded bra or one that lifts your sagging breasts up? That's deceptive. Do you use teeth whitener or have veneers? That's deceptive too. If you carry a fake handbag that's even more deceptive than having surgery. At least in fixing your nose or adding to your breasts, it's still your nose and breasts. A fake bag is a fake bag, it's all fake and you're trying to pass it off as real, or you would've gotten a bag you could afford!

What's real anymore and where is the line? Nobody can answer that but you. Maybe you are considering plastic surgery—maybe breast augmentation, a facelift, or a nose job. If you've ever felt unhappy with any body part and don't mind the pain involved, then go ahead and fix it. I would just caution you that it must be done for you and only you. Have several consultations, but don't do anything until you have done all the healthy inner work to help you get okay with yourself as you are! This isn't going to fix anything going on that is affecting your sense of self-worth. Cosmetic surgery should be considered nothing more than an enhancement of an already perfect you. If you feel insecure before surgery you will feel insecure after surgery. Getting new breasts may make your husband (or any men you might date in the future) fall all over you, but those men won't stick around if your heart hasn't healed beneath those new, fabulous breasts.

There are many non-surgical ways to improve your physical appearance, such as exercise, healthy diet, good sleep, meditation, etc., which we will go into later. If you really love yourself, get whatever you want done for you, and don't let anyone else's judgment affect your decision. This is about you. You will always be the love of your life. Friends, lovers, and even your children will come and go; you're the only one who is staying around. If you want to hang out with you for the rest of your life with a new nose or bigger breasts, by all means, go for it.

EAT IT

Do you like your Cap'n Crunch® or Raisin Bran®? How do you feel about your weight? If you think that you could lose a few pounds go for it, but please don't ever use the word "diet"! It makes me cringe. Some people cringe at the word "fuck," I cringe at the word "diet." The thing is *fuck* works; diets don't! Cutting your food portions in half and not eating yummy, fattening comfort foods works. Caring about your weight is essential when you are trying to feel good about yourself, trying to fix your marriage, getting through a divorce, or once you dive into the dating pool if you chose to divorce. If you are past the age of fourteen, you know boys/men really care about weight! I didn't make the rule. It is what it is!

But, weight loss must be for you and nobody else. If you have an eating disorder, zero self-discipline, or a medical issue, you are going to need some help from a doctor, nutritionist, trainer, or hypnotist. I know it can be difficult to succeed in our "I want it right now" world, but be patient so smart, healthy food choices can have the impact on your overall wellbeing that they are designed to have. There is no quick-fix that won't have significant side-effects or downsides to it, even if you get the rapid results you're after. Your long-term health depends on being willing to stick with a plan for making good choices and honoring your body's nutritional needs. Just make sure you are keeping your doctor in the loop on any changes you incorporate so they can check to make sure you are getting in all the vitamins and minerals your body needs to function at its best and enjoy your life in the process.

ROSANNA

Rosanna was pretty overweight and her husband left her for a woman he worked with. When this happened, she dove into exercising, watched her food intake, started getting her nails done, got some highlights, and, after she dropped forty pounds, bought some new clothes to show off her new figure. Sure enough, after seeing the fabulous changes in her, Rosanna's husband came crawling back, realizing this new woman wasn't who he wanted, that he wanted his family back. She told him to go fuck himself in a lovely way.

The point of the story is that the best revenge is taking care of yourself and being happy with whatever life throws at you. She knew if she made some outer beauty changes it would grab men's attention. Plus, it boosted her confidence and she landed a great guy! (FYI, I have tons of stories like this.) Men are triggered visually! They want a woman on their arm next to them to show off and be proud of. Just like you want a good-looking man who is a good provider. Rosanna started taking care of herself and feeling great in her own skin. She could have taken him back if she had felt it was best for her family, but she now had the confidence to demand better for herself, and her husband learned the hard way not to take her for granted.

LET'S GET PHYSICAL

Physical, you wanna get physical? You need to listen to your body talk about what it needs, and I can't stress enough how important exercise is when you are going through a life transition! Exercise has been proven to give you more energy and focus and to lift depression. If you hate exercising, find exercises you enjoy—physical activity that is easy and fun for you—so you'll keep doing them. For exercise lovers, challenge yourself or try a different type of workout. You can go online and find new classes you may love.

Exercise is also a great distraction; it takes your mind off your misery. Group exercise can offer enjoyable social opportunities—meeting new people is always fun. You may meet someone in the same boat you're in and gain a great friend to add to your support network.

Remember: If you have time to talk on the phone to a friend, you have time to walk. I made a rule for myself that I can't talk on the phone to friends, unless I'm walking. All that time you spend talking to friends on the phone will turn into time well spent if you are moving while you do it. If I'm not talking on the phone when I walk, I listen to TED talks. I often find I'm so interested in the talk that I keep walking longer than I planned and, at the end, I've learned something. And please don't get intimidated by runners and joggers passing you by. I have another rule: I don't run unless someone is chasing me. I have a little game I play sometimes when I see someone jogging. I imagine what that person is running from, what they stole, or make up some other excuse for why they would be moving that fast. Finding ways to entertain yourself makes exercise much more tolerable.

SEASONS CHANGE

Unless you live in Southern California or a similar climate, seasons change. People also change; so, the first thing you must do after making all these outer beauty changes is work on the inner beauty. It's important to do this for yourself, to reconnect with the things that enrich your life as an individual, though you may find that a happy by-product of this work is renewed interest from your partner. If you start looking like a pretty Flower and get busy improving yourself, your husband may step it up to draw your attention back to him. If he's a good man he will love the new you and have the highest respect for you as you try to make some self-improvements on the inside as well, and hopefully on the outside if he's fashion challenged.

PRIDE (IN THE NAME OF LOVE)

One Flower comes in the name of love. She may come or she may go. This Flower may try to justify why she wants to leave her marriage, but until she is willing to make all these adjustments to help her find herself again and try to fix what is broken in her marriage, has she really acted out of love? Have some pride, pretty Flower, and remember that you too are in this partnership and it's not all about what he needs to do to change. You should want to be the best person you can be, no matter what your marital status is, so get to work and see what kinds of rewards come your way.

WHEN I SEE YOU SMILE

It's really true that a smile can help you face the world under any circumstances, whether it's the smile you see on someone else's face or the one you wear on your own. Think about it, your kids have sports and dance and other extra-curricular activities and, unless you are one of those parents who pressures them to be Type-A personalities from infancy, these activities are things that bring them joy. Don't you deserve the same? Before you decide to leave your marriage, take up a hobby you've always wanted to try, such as gardening or an art class, which is very relaxing and gets you outside of the rut you're in. (Maybe avoid something like knife throwing if you're dealing with anger issues at the moment. Kickboxing might be a better choice for working out frustrations.) If you're not sure what hobby suits you, sign up for a few classes and try whatever intrigues you until you land on something you connect with.

Settle on a hobby and give it your all for a few months . . . and give yourself permission to suck for a while until you get the hang of it. I had always danced when I was younger, but I gave it up when I was married. After my divorce I went back to ballet class. It made me feel alive again. I had years of catching up to do and wanted to quit, but I was determined to do the splits and turns the other girls were doing and refused to give up. Whether you stay in your marriage or choose to leave, discovering new interests is a gift you need to give yourself.

ALL NIGHT PASSION

Okay, so I know Alisha is talking about a different kind of passion than what I mean—one we will get into in another part of the book—but feeling passionate about anything is a great driving force for living fully. Hobbies and passions may seem similar, but there is a difference, as passions can evolve into life pursuits. This is important because, if you've been staying home raising the kids, the harsh reality is that when they go to school (or even worse, leave the nest) you are going to feel all alone. Your life can't be centered on your kids and husband if you want to avoid losing yourself. You have to have other things that give you happiness and fulfill you.

What about painting? Let's be honest, Picasso is overrated. I've seen some of my friend's kid's second grade artwork that looks just as good. So, don't tell yourself you can't do it. I live near the Los Angeles Contemporary Museum of Art. They have classes all the time and they aren't that expensive. Give it a try. You may discover a hidden talent you never knew you had.

Maybe pottery is more your thing. If you watched Demi Moore in the movie *Ghost* it probably put turning mud into a vase in a whole new light. You may not be visited by any celestial beings or meet a hot man like Patrick Swayze, but you could get a fun new coffee cup or handy ashtray out of it.

Did you ever think about going to the batting cages?

It's a great place to get your anger out. Hitting a ball is empowering and makes you release some anger energy; also, it's usually full of men who would be more than glad to help you. A woman hitting balls at the batting cages is like seeing the rare straight man getting a pedicure at the nail salon.

RIO

Her name was Rio and she was married to Harry for forty years and they just kind of grew apart. He worked all the time and loved to play golf. She did a lot of charity work and had a lot of friends, so she always stayed pretty busy. Unfortunately, they just couldn't seem to get on the same page, no matter how hard she tried. Part of the problem was that Harry was super stubborn and didn't want to change at all.

Rio always loved to paint, so she started to paint again to take her mind off her consideration of divorce. She got so involved in painting that he actually got a little jealous of it and started trying to get her attention back. Men need love and attention too. She had stopped doing a lot of the little things she had always done for him because she was so busy with her new hobby. As a result, he started doing things that he used to do to win her affection. They started to appreciate each other again. In taking her focus off him and putting it on herself, she saved her marriage.

MEXICAN RADIO

If you find yourself in Tijuana, you're going to be wishing you'd picked up a new language. These days, everyone is speaking Spanish, and maybe you understand just a little. Learning it will be beneficial in lots of ways.

As Americans we have come to expect that we can travel anywhere and count on them knowing English, so think about how grateful you are when they do. Now, put yourself in the shoes of someone who doesn't speak English. Wouldn't you appreciate and enjoy being able to communicate with someone in your native language, especially if it isn't one that is spoken all around the world.

Learning new languages exposes you to new cultures as well and that is a good thing. Broadening your horizons and becoming more cultured not only makes you a more interesting person, it could be a great excuse for you and your husband to take a special trip and rekindle some of the romance.

FASCINATION STREET

Let's take a walk down Fascination Street and explore the things that interest you and might be something to build a career on or expand your existing work. Have you thought about going back to college? If you've always regretted not finishing your degree, start investigating what it would take to work on it at night or while the kids are at school. Maybe there is additional certification that would help you advance in your career and you've been putting it off.

There is never a bad time to learn new things and explore opportunities to better yourself; but, let's be honest, it would be so much easier doing it while you're married than when you're divorced, juggling things alone, and desperate to find work to help support yourself and the kids. I highly recommend going back to school before your divorce, not after, when you're stressed financially and have kids to take care of alone. Don't think your ex will stick around and do the right thing for his children. If he marries someone woman who lives far away, or decides to take a new job far away and become a Disneyland dad, you may be on your own. It will be too hard to go back to school.

I can't guarantee this will fix what is wrong in your marriage. There is always the chance your husband is the controlling type who doesn't like the idea of you growing;

but, if he's like that, taking a step like this to protect and equip yourself is even more important. However, any man who is at all secure in himself will beam with pride over his wife as she walks across the stage to accept that long-awaited and hard-earned diploma. Why not explore the possibilities?

SHE WORKS HARD FOR THE MONEY

Whether you are staying home with your kids or going to a job outside the home, there is no doubt you work hard and deserve to be treated right. But, if you're feeling unhappy in your marriage, having a job to go to can give you a sense of purpose or at least a break from being at home all day to get a different perspective. If you have small kids, child care is likely to consume most of what you earn, but don't think of a part-time job as being for the money so much as for your mental health. Having a little paycheck in your hand with your name on it can make you feel like you're contributing in a different way in the relationship. Plus, you could meet some great people and have a chance to have some grownup conversation in your day.

I know that being a mother may be one of the most important things you do in life and being with your children and nurturing them is really important work. But, I also know that moms are women too and they need to be able to be adults and do things that exercise their brains more than what they get from preschooler TV or playground gossip. Giving your kids your best only comes from giving yourself a chance to be fully you.

DOCTOR, DOCTOR

You may be wondering if anyone can see you burning, burning with confusion, fear, frustration, or anger and be wanting some help. This final category of personal work is probably going to be the hardest for most of you because it means really digging deep to figure out what's going on with you. You might already have a counselor you visit regularly, and if you do, maybe it's time to start doing the hard work they've been asking you to do. If not, ask around and find someone reputable and prepare yourself before you go in to make this about improving you, not about finding a sympathetic ear for your complaints about your husband.

It's a fatal mistake many people make, thinking that they will find happiness when they leave a marriage, but if you are unhappy in a relationship, I can promise you that without finding yourself again and doing some real soul searching, you are not going to be any happier single. In fact, you'll probably be even more miserable. Sometimes we get a bit lost and just need some direction. If you can sit down and write out a list of all the things you like, want, and need, that's a great start. Everyone could benefit from some therapy at different points in their lives for coping with tough situations. The insights you get from someone with proper training and experience can be a lifesaver . . . and maybe a marriage saver too.

SO ALIVE

Do you feel alive? I mean really alive? If you've been working on improving yourself inside and out, you should be overflowing with energy and excitement about life. If something is still missing, it might be that you need to get outside of yourself now and do something to improve the world around you. It may start with your home environment. It might mean volunteering and serving others in need. Either way, doing something to get your mind off of yourself and your troubles can be the best thing you do for your relationship.

HAZY SHADE OF WINTER

GOODBYE TO YOU

If you're looking around and the leaves are brown and you are feeling gloomy, whether it's just the weather or something more, you don't have to wait for Spring to do some serious Spring Cleaning. You might think I'm crazy here, but if the thought of exercise really does not appeal to you, another healthy outlet is a deep cleaning on your house! There is nothing like having closets purged and organized, baseboards and ceiling corners cleaned of cobwebs, and a floor so clean you could eat off of it to give you a new lease on life.

Turn the music up or put on a TED talk and move, mopping the floor, dusting, vacuuming, and scrubbing. It's really good for you because you're expending energy and contracting muscles; plus, being in a really clean environment helps you clear your mind as well. I know it may sound stupid, but it works. When you are feeling dissatisfied or unhappy, declutter and get your world back in order. It may not fix your marriage, but it will certainly help you think more clearly about what the right thing is for your situation.

WE ARE THE WORLD

Has the time come for you to heed a certain call? I don't mean to sound harsh, pretty Flower, but sometimes all you really need is a little perspective and a few minutes of thinking about someone other than yourself. Volunteering your time to those who are less fortunate and need your help could be the key to saving your marriage.

Community service can reframe what's important in life for you. Maybe you help out the children at your kids' school or you find a neighborhood improvement project that can use a helping hand. Try visiting a nursing home and talking with an older woman who has lost her husband after years of marriage; she will tell you marriage isn't easy and how important love and family are. Volunteering at women's shelters where women are actually traumatized by their husbands will help you appreciate your husband who simply forgot your anniversary. What about at a hospice center? You may see your situation in a totally different light when you visit with people who are dying and saying goodbye to loved ones.

Maybe you have always loved animals and working with them as a volunteer is something you'd like to do as a hobby. As you do that you could discover your passion for protecting animals runs deeper than that and you decide you want to find work that allows you to do more or you become an activist for animal rights. We need people out there fighting for our furry companions!

Learning to stop taking time, health, resources, and people for granted will help you reevaluate the aspects of your marriage that are making you unhappy and look for more positive solutions than divorce.

FOOLIN'

Oh, I just gotta know if you are making excuses, like finances, time, or the approval of your husband are stopping you from doing things to improve your life. Excuses are excuses, and you're just foolin' yourself. People who really want something will always find a way to do it. Value yourself enough to give this gift to yourself. When you do things to rediscover who you are, or find yourself for the first time, everyone around you benefits, so don't think of this as being selfish. If you did all these things all along you might not be so unhappy. These were things you made time for when you were single and they made you so vibrant and appealing that your future husband couldn't resist making you his wife. You will have to do most of these things when you are single; so, why not start doing them now?

THE TIDE IS HIGH

Maybe the tide is high in your relationship and you feel the water rising around you and you think you should be moving on. Don't be the girl who gives up just like that, especially if you have children. See if some of these changes made a difference in how you feel and how he is treating you. All relationships ebb and flow, and your natural tendency is to want to stay in the good, perfect moments. But, pretty Flower, that's not realistic. Besides, how do you really appreciate the good times if you don't know the bad? How do you grow as a person if things never change? How do you learn all those delicious lessons that we all need to experience to become a better person in all areas of our lives? Maybe, your kids are smaller now and things are hectic and hard, but think about what happens when they get older and you and your husband can go places again and travel together when you get older.

In today's instant gratification world, we often view things as disposable if they aren't working for us at any given moment. We've slipped into this five-second attention span mode where even Amazon Now, with its drone delivery service isn't fast enough. And we want it perfect. If it's not perfect or didn't meet our expectations, we return it and try another option. Sometimes the product was just fine, but maybe it wasn't exactly how we envisioned or it had a minor flaw that doesn't affect the way it works. We tend to look for the same unrealistic ideal in our marriages. If it requires some assembly (work), we'd just as soon scrap it. If it's broken, we want it fixed ASAP or we want a replacement. But, we can't treat our relationships like something we get off the internet.

If your marriage can be saved, isn't it worth it to do everything in your power to make that happen? Riding out the rough seas of relationships can be really rewarding because it can make you stronger as a couple. And, if it just can't be saved, at least you have a great head start on the things you are going to have to do for healing after you are divorced. Life is forcing you to change yourself, doing it now will be so much easier.

DE DO DO DO DE DA DA DA

I have one more thing to say to you. I talk to a lot of women whose husbands left and don't want to work things out. He's already out the door and playing with other fish in the sea. Please note: There is absolutely nothing that you can do to change that. He's having the time of his life and is in the honeymoon phase with a new woman or several new women. Unfortunately, he may see you as interfering with his fun right now. You're a reminder that he's doing the wrong thing for you and his family. You will look desperate and pathetic if you are texting him, calling him, or, God forbid, crying to him. And that will only push him away.

If you want him back, the best (and probably only) way to do that is to work on yourself. If you look beyond fabulous and get all of your shit together, then let him know you love him and want the marriage to work. But, make sure he knows you're not waiting around for him; that's the way to get his attention. If you are looking like butter, he may realize what he lost and come back. Look fab and live your life. If your husband wakes up and makes the effort, you win. If you work on you and get the most out of your life and meet a new guy along the way, you win again! I've seen this happen many, many times. Okay, that's all I have to say to you in this chapter.

Let's move on to Chapter 3 and see what we can do next to keep your soon-to-be-ex-husband your husband. I know you just want to get divorced and you're thinking, *Don't keep me hanging on, set me free,* but let's just give your ex a fighting chance if he's willing.

Chapter 3
MAN IN THE MIRROR

Okay, let's see if he can make a change for once in his life. If he wants to put this marriage in a better place, he needs to look at himself and make some changes too. And we all know how men love to change, learn, and grow. I have to say it's becoming more acceptable for men to start reading self-help books and to get some therapy. If he doesn't want to lose you he may be all on board. Hopefully, if you have applied the self-love tips I gave you in the last chapter, this chapter may not even be necessary. Your husband may be so shocked from all of your changes that he has stepped up already. But, if he hasn't noticed anything yet, you may have to start being a smart Flower and making a lot of suggestions for change in a loving way. Let's start by trying to get your husband to do some things to save the marriage. Don't nag, suggest! If you've already decided to get divorced, skip over this chapter and move on to Phase 2. Don't waste your time; but, this info might be good for your next relationship.

DON'T DO ME LIKE THAT
Baby, Baby, don't do him like that and bring up divorce. I want to be clear, don't say the word "divorce"; it is super serious and emotionally charged and can shut down any useful conversation before you even get started. It shouldn't be thrown on the table unless he refuses to work with you on the things you want and need that are recommended in this chapter. If he has given up and doesn't want to try to make things better, you can tell him you are at a make-or-break moment and divorce is where you're headed if something doesn't change. See if that lights the fire of change.

People throw *divorce* around way too often as a scare

tactic, and it shouldn't be used that way. You took a vow for life and going back on that shouldn't even be considered as an option unless you're pretty much done already. Let's hope the man you love and the man who loves you wants to try to get the love back on track and work on the marriage too. He doesn't need to know your plan; he just needs to see you're changing and making an effort to grow and that you want him to grow with you.

WHAT I LIKE ABOUT YOU

So, what do you like about him? Is it that he really knows how to dance? Is it the way he holds you tight? When you've reached the point that you're considering ending your marriage it's important to reassess what your relationship has meant to you and why you were in it to begin with.

I'm going to ask you to stop everything you're doing or planning right now and make a list of all the great things about your husband. You may find you're having to reach for things, and it's okay if you're at that point. If you've been growing apart for a while, you may have forgotten all the little things that made you want to build a life with him. But, you know he has a lot of good qualities, whether you want to acknowledge them right now or not. Even if you have to start with stupid or silly things like he takes quick showers or keeps his car clean in order to get started, go ahead. It will get the flow going and you'll find your way to more substantial things. Maybe break out the old pictures of when you were young and in love, remember all those good time. If you're especially angry or checked out right now, talk to a friend who has known him a long time. They probably see him in a different light than you do in your current state of mind and can help you recall some of his better qualities.

Here, I'm going to get you started with some suggestions:

1. He's a good provider.
2. He's faithful.
3. He's kind to others.
4. He's funny.
5. He's a hard worker.
6. He knows how to fix things around the house.
7. He's thoughtful.
8. He's got a great family.
9. He's got big brown eyes.
10. He's got a big penis.

Once you make your list, I want you to focus on those qualities for the next month—thirty days of only thinking about his positive qualities. And have fun with this. Don't look at it as a chore or something you are forced to do. Remember, this is someone you love or have loved— someone you chose— so enjoy reminding yourself of why you did. You will likely have a day where he puts a nearly empty milk carton back in the fridge or something else insignificant that triggers your irritation all over again. That's okay; just start the thirty days over and try to find something endearing, or at least humorous, in his quirks rather than just annoyance.

Also, during this time, keep a journal and write down how you did each day. Laugh at yourself if you got irritated because the toilet seat wasn't down or he threw clothes on the floor or came home late from work. Your attitude is "I"- centered—I've got great hobbies and good friends, and I have a good guy because he's a hard worker, he's funny, he's kind, etc. Keep everything about him super positive.

JUST LIKE HEAVEN

Remember how happy you were when things were good? How it was just like a dream? Over the thirty days of focusing on his good qualities, try to recapture some of the heaven of young love by doing something fun each day, such as:

1. Write about the day you met him. What did you do? What was he wearing? Why did you like him? Did he make you laugh? What made you agree to a second date?

2. Write about how happy you were when you were dating. Write down all the fun things you did together—your favorite hangouts, meeting his family for the first time, vacations you took.

3. Write about the day he asked you to marry him. How did he do it? Who did you call first? How did you feel?

4. Write about your wedding day. Describe all the good things that happened that day. Who came from a long distance? Who were your best man and maid of honor?

5. Write about the honeymoon. Where did you go and for how long? How was the sex? Did you try great food? Did you leave the room at all to see the area?

6. Write about the day you moved into your first apartment or bought your first house. Was it tiny? In a bad part of town? How did you decorate it?

7. Write about the life you've built together. Did you have children together? How did he handle it when you went into labor? How did you choose their names? Or did you have pets together?

These are supposed to bring up fond memories and good feelings. If you have a bad experience associated with one of these questions, skip it and move on to the next, or try to find something positive to say on the subject.

When my ex and I were dating, we hardly had any money and we couldn't afford a kitchen table. We ate on my step. (No, not my front stoop, my exercise step from the 80s. I still use it as my work out most days.) We were young, broke, and happy. When he pulls some horrible shit over the years, I try to think of that. It's one of my happiest memories with my ex, eating on my step. I can remember how handsome he looked, and the amazing conversations we used to have. I try not to let the fact he lied more than Pinocchio and had more affairs than Tiger Woods taint my memory of eating on my step. Plus, I can never hate him, only his behavior, because he gave me the two best kids in the world, and I will always love him for that. You can choose what to focus on— the good or the bad—it's your choice. Choose what is better for you; they are your thoughts.

STEPPIN' OUT

I know how easy it is to use the excuses that you don't have time or money for date night. Do you have time and money for a divorce? The average divorce costs around $15,000, which doesn't include moving expenses, time off from work, and medical expenses from the stress. I'm telling you now, find it! Charge it if you have to. It will cost you less than a divorce. Or get creative and come up with something free and fun to do together. In fact, the more effort you put into dating, the more you'll reconnect to why you want to spend time together and remember the things you used to enjoy doing when you were young and in love but broke. You're going to be dating anyway you look at it, whether it's your husband or a stranger that you meet online if you get divorced.

Tell your husband that you would like to go to a specific restaurant where you have great memories of your relationship or somewhere you both will be happy. Make it special and dress up, but change things up a bit and give your look an update. If you don't ever show cleavage, show those girls off. If you don't usually wear short skirts, show off your fabulous legs. If you don't wear a lot of makeup, be a little bolder, you PYT (Pretty Young Thing). Make this fun for both of you! Turn this into a game for you—a game to reignite your husband's love and attention and to find your love for him again. Dating is a game you will play if you get divorced, so why not play this game first? I guarantee this game is more fun! Do this once a week thing during the 30-day positivity period and see what happens.

JOHNNIE ARE YOU QUEER

How's the sex life? Have you been asking if his love is for real when the lights are low? Having sex with your spouse is what makes you more than roommates. And while you may not be as randy as you were when you were young, a non-existent sex life could be an indication of problems. I have known of several friend's husbands who came out after many years of marriage. This is a reality for some women!

It's really unusual for the sexual chemistry to be super strong decades into the marriage. The honeymoon phase of relationships tends to be the time of great sex and intimacy. And, after the years have passed, the craziness of raising kids, working long hours, and the dumb chores we all have to do every week kills the once thriving libido we used to have. But, sex is a vital component in a healthy relationship; it involves intimacy that only you two share, which bonds you together like Krazy clue. This is why affairs are so detrimental to a marriage—it's the one thing that you are supposed to only share together that no one else is supposed to experience with you. When the sex breaks down, everything else in the relationship can really suffer, but an active sex life can keep couples together. We all want to feel desirable and have the reassurance that we are sexy and turn our partner on.

Remember, sex isn't just a physical thing; it's an emotional connection as well. Having an orgasm gives you a rush of endorphins and you will never be closer to him than in the moments when you've just had sex. Getting your groove on may help you get the love back faster than anything else you do. Obviously, this doesn't fix everything; but, after sex you may feel differently about him and find a little of the connection that you've lost. Try spicing things up with something like Tantric Sex, which is a slow form of meditative sex that increases intimacy and is supposed to lead to a very powerful orgasm. Who doesn't want a powerful orgasm? If you haven't had sex in years, he may think you're insane if you bring this up right away, but in time it could really help get your marriage back together. It's fun reading about it anyway, and if you divorce him and get a new guy, you will have some knowledge about something very intimate, fun, and explosive!

GRACELAND

At this point, your husband is probably taking notice and realizing something is up, and he probably wouldn't be surprised if you walked in and said, "I'm going to Graceland, honey." He may have called up his friends or his mom, saying that you've really changed. "Diane got highlights/Botox/is learning to play the drums/got a part time job. Do you think there's someone else? She seems really happy!"

This is when you can tell him that the two of you should go somewhere romantic near you. But don't give him a chance to come up with excuses; just pick a spot and tell him the date you want to go. But, don't do it for him! Let him be the man and tell him it's time for him to start participating. I know you are probably afraid he won't do it, but with praise and ego stroking you should be able to get him to think it's his idea and thank him for being so smart and proactive. You're a smart Flower; you can do this!

Start with a fun weekend away! See how that goes. You've been dating your husband for a bit, going out to dinners, trying to spend more time with him; hopefully this little romantic weekend away will light a nice fire for the two of you, and not just the fireplace in your romantic suite. If this weekend goes well, you can move on to a romantic week getaway.

KEY LARGO

Going to one of those all-inclusive resorts where you can get there fast and then take it slow could be just what you need to really reconnect with your husband. It's sunny and the drinks are free and everyone is a happy Flower. Go and be his Caribbean queen for a week. These trips are not as expensive as you might think. You can always find a good deal. Again, it's still less expensive than a divorce. I know you're thinking he's not going to do this because men only step up for drastic measures if they think they may lose you. If he does say he doesn't have time to go and makes a fuss about it, no worries! Tell him you'll ask a friend to go with you. Don't nag or act like you are disappointed! Seriously, take the trip alone if you have to, and have a great time; but, I bet he changes his mind and goes.

If you divorce him you will be going on trips alone anyway, so you'll need to start getting used to single life now. FYI, I've never been on a trip alone when I didn't meet someone fabulous to hang out with (male or female). If you fall back in love again, or at least start to rediscover those feelings, how great for you, your kids, your family, your friends, your health and for the overall commitment of marriage. If it doesn't go well, you need to really dig deep within yourself and see if you should consider divorce more seriously, or try a bit harder to say your marriage. But, before you pass the Dutchie to the left hand side, let's look at some stories.

DIANE

Diane and her husband, Jack, had the best marriage I've

ever seen. I asked her their secret and she told me they had sex all the time and always put each other first no matter what. They had two kids they really loved, but they loved each other first and always had date nights. They continued to take trips just for the two of them for valuable bonding time together.

I remember calling her one time and asking her what she did the night before and her answer was, "I fucked Jack in an elevator after dinner." Her skin always had a continuous glow, not from a good skin care regimen, but from a consistent orgasm regimen. They could've let life and kids bring their marriage down, but they didn't. They always put each other first, even when things got rough. She told me, "It's your choice to keep things alive or let it die." Her husband certainly wasn't perfect and had a lot of flaws, but she chose happiness.

I will say that she didn't have to work outside the home during the marriage, and when woman have a full-time job, kids, a house, and a husband who all require something of her, it's hard to do it all. Diane had time to go to the gym during the day, get groceries to make dinner, and attend to little details that make life special. They loved having nice dinners together with the kids, and she had time for things a lot of woman don't have time to do. Not having time like this can cause your marriage to suffer and a lot of times it leads to divorce. That's why it's so hard to stay married nowadays. Women are expected to be Superwoman. Some women can handle it and are happy, but some can't. Unrealistic expectations of another human, or of yourself, will kill a marriage. Jack could afford to take care of his family, and wanted Diane home. He knew his needs wouldn't be met if she had a full time job outside the home, so he found a way to create that kind of life for them. Jack is a smart guy—I hear a lot of men in 2017 say they want their wife working full-time, but then get pissed off that she didn't cook dinner, the house is a mess, the kids need baths, and he's not getting the sex that night. They can't have it all. #YoureNotSuperwoman

OH, SHERRIE

Sherrie's husband cheated on her when they were in their late twenties. She didn't want to get divorced and wanted to work things out. I don't know how this couple survived and is as happy as they are now. After he cheated on her Sherrie was angry and heartbroken and really embarrassed. She didn't have sex with him for years and put him through a living hell. Most men would have left, but he must've really loved her to endure the shit she put him through. (I think he deserved every bit of punishment she gave him and it helped her feel better.) In time, they started to have sex again and he became a different man—a good, loving, moral, standup guy for his wife and children.

They are in their sixties now, and she told me that she's so happy that she stayed with him. She has the best marriage now and their love holds on. The kids are grown, they love their grandchildren, they travel, and they are spending those golden years with a lot of love and respect. The affair strengthened their marriage and he never cheated again because Sherrie held him accountable and made him pay in ways he wouldn't forget. I think that's how you know if the marriage can stay together after an affair, Since, he was willing to take her shit and took responsibility for his wrongdoings, the marriage was saved. Only you know what is best for you, and you have to honor your feelings on whatever path you chose. I know you will make the right decision either way, because you're a smart Flower! But, if he cheats again, lovingly kick him the hell out!

FAITH

Sometimes you gotta have faith; you just gotta have faith that he will turn back into the guy you fell in love with. What are your spiritual beliefs? Do you belong to a church or religious organization? If so, please reach out to these people for support or counseling. They can help a lot. Don't be embarrassed that you are having problems. Every marriage has problems! When people say they don't have any problems in their relationship, they're lying. You know that! We all irritate each other and get on each other's nerves once in a while, and the longer you spend time with someone the more they tend to annoy you.

I don't think livin' on a prayer is realistic, but pastors or religious leaders want your marriage to work and, not only are they trained to deal with pretty much any relationship issue, they have seen it all and have helped many others through similar situations. They are rooting for you to work out and find your love for each other again. They know having a solid family foundation for you and your children really is in your best interests.

DR. FEELGOOD
So is Dr. Feelgood someone you need to see to make you feel alright? I've already suggested individual counseling as a way to work on your own stuff, but maybe it's time to consider couples counseling. I'm all for martial counseling if you both are willing, but only after you do all the stuff I recommended. The reason I don't suggest it first is because I'm trying to save you some money and headache. They are probably going to tell you to do a lot of the same stuff I have. And, if none of it has worked, you probably have bigger, deeper issues that will require a lot of sessions—at least two or three times per week—and fifty minutes of talking can't really solve much, especially if you guys are going reluctantly as a last ditch effort.

Bottom line here is, if you both are really dedicated and want marriage counseling to work, it will! But, you both need to be on board 100 percent or you might as well call it quits and move on to another relationship and start fresh with all the wisdom you gained from this one and what you learned in this book.

TIME AFTER TIME

I think all marital counselors should be like my four-foot, outspoken, Italian grandmother. She would yell at both of you considering getting divorced and tell you you're stupid and selfish that you let the marriage get to this point, and to go home and love each other, take care of your kids, and have a lot of sex. She was married to my Poppy for forty years, and if she fell, he was there to catch her. When he died that was it for her. He was the love of her life. She lived twenty-five years after he died and missed him and loved him every day. And believe me he was not perfect. She accepted him for who he was. She could bitch about him all day if she wanted to, but she chose to see all of his good qualities instead of his bad and loved him for who he was, faults and all.

My Nanny married my grandpa when she was super young. They were dirt poor. These days, marrying young and dirt poor is a recipe for divorce, but back in their day things were different. People appreciated things that they had and the people in their lives more than they do now. They were married for four years before she would have children because my Nanny didn't want to have a baby without having a refrigerator first, and it took them four years to save up. My Poppy would wash her back every night in the bathtub (this was before there were showers). My cousin Lois once asked her the secret to her loving, strong marriage, and she said it was due to their having sex every night for ten years in a row. Everyone wants this type of love, which only happens when you are lucky enough to find and marry the right man, and then choose to love him through all the good and bad.

I CAN'T GO FOR THAT (NO CAN DO)

I'm going to suggest something now that may sound really out there, and you may think, *No way! I can't go for that!* But, just hear me out. I believe that before anyone really considers divorcing, they should do a three-month separation and try online dating. Go on at least three online dating sites and go on three dates per week. Be honest about your age, height, and weight. You are not doing yourself any favors by misleading people and you won't appreciate it when you find out they have done the same. Also, tell the truth about your status—that you're separated. Don't worry, thinking nobody will date you because you're separated; people date married people nowadays like it's okay. If I had a dollar for every married man who hit on me and my single friends over the years, we could feed a small village in a third world country for the next ten years. The morals and rules around dating/marriage have changed significantly. The reason I want you to go on a few dates is that it will give you a sense of what's out there, and you might find you are better off trying to recapture the flame with your husband. Please remember to be safe while you are dating online. The people you are meeting are strangers, and not everyone has the best intentions for you. I really hope you can work it out with your husband if you have children; but, if you can't, I hope that you find someone to take away the heartache if that is what is meant to be for you, and you don't go through the horror that most single women go through finding their second or third husband. Most women are very happy being single women for a very good reason. Skip down to Chapter 8 and read the dating chapter before you head out there into the dating scene, and be prepared to go on dates like I had.

IT'S THE END OF THE WORD AS WE KNOW IT

And you feel fine. If you feel 99 percent confident that divorce is the right decision for you, and you've decided to move on, at least you can say you tried; you really tried. You won't be able to mess with yourself later on, thinking that you woulda, coulda, shoulda done this or that. You tried! If you followed my suggestions, you did everything you possibly could to save your marriage. You will know deep in your heart you tried everything, so you can't run a full-blown guilt trip on yourself when your life is falling apart from all the difficulties that come with divorce. You will have made the choice with full awareness knowing all the potential consequences of your decision.

I really hope that you don't need to read the divorce section of this book; but, if you do, I'm going to guide you in the only way I know how—with brutal honesty, a dose of tough love, and some really fabulous 80s flashbacks to make your transition from Mrs. to Ms. a little lighter.

Phase 2

ANOTHER ONE BITES THE DUST

If you have moved into Phase 2, then it means another one's gone. And another one's gone, if this was your second marriage. Another one bites the dust. The reality check I gave you to try and save your marriage didn't work. So, now I have to ask, "Are you ready for this?" In this section we are going to cover all the things you need to consider as you move toward and through a divorce. I'm going to give it to you straight about what to expect emotionally from the upheaval you are about to endure. I'm also going to give you the kind of practical advice I give to my clients and friends. And, the last chapter in this section holds the secrets for surviving this nightmare and finding your way to being happy and satisfied.

Chapter 4
WHEN DOVES CRY

There are different reasons you or your ex are going to leave each other standing alone in a world that can be cold. We're going to be talking through some of the really hard stuff, though I hope by the end of the chapter you'll feel a little lighter and ready to do this thing from a place of strength and hope. If you have reached the point where divorce just seems inevitable and the only way out of your situation, you may find yourself tempted to just torch the thing and walk away. But, there are ways to get divorced without destroying everyone in your path.

One of the first things you can do to avoid this is prepare yourself for a tidal wave of emotions. Understanding them and being better equipped for how to deal with them will make a big difference in how you survive this major life change. I can't promise you it will be pain free. And, nothing I say here is going to have an impact on how your ex will behave. Hurt cray-cray people will want to fight in court and take everything from you. Hurt healthy people will want to end it as soon as possible and not spend a ton on lawyers and, more important, do what is right for their children. I can only give you tips for how to conduct yourself with dignity and self-respect.

Having survived it twice, I want you to learn from my mistakes and avoid some of the common errors I've seen women make while going through a divorce. The way you handle your divorce will show a lot about who you are and what is important to you, stay rational and always remember this is a business transaction for your financial future.

TEAR US APART

I bet when your two worlds collided you never thought they would be torn apart. There are a lot of reasons people decide to end a marriage and they range from the petty and self-serving to the urgent and life-threatening. The reason I spent so much time in Phase 1 talking about ways to avoid divorce is because I believe in marriage and don't want to see people jump too quickly to divorce as a solution for things that can be overcome. I don't think I can say enough in this book that if you are in a dangerous situation with an abusive or adulterous spouse, you don't need to put yourself at greater risk by trying to stay and work things out. But, if, after reading through this section, you find that some of the reasons you are considering divorce are something you can work on, go back and read Phase 1 again and see if you can salvage your relationship. That said, let's look at the most common reasons people give for seeking divorce.

NO ONE IS TO BLAME

Okay, I'm going to go ahead and say it: Irreconcilable differences is a lame excuse that most people use instead of saying, "I'm just not into it anymore." Yes, sometimes it's a nice way of saying we made a big mistake and just don't belong together, and if that is the case, you are better off getting out; although, I hope you figured this out before you had kids. I do think a lot of these differences are things that can be overcome and you can salvage a marriage if you just try to see past the fact that maybe life isn't as glamorous as you thought it would be or the fires of passion don't burn as hotly as they used to.

There are times when the things that divide you really are too big to overcome; but, in most cases, they are things that were there from the beginning and if you'd taken a little more time to get to know them, you'd have seen these issues before walking down the aisle. Or, if you did see them, and foolishly thought you could change your man, you might have benefited from taking a breath to get over your wedding fever. I know I'm being a little harsh here, Flower, and it's rarely useful to say, "I told you so," when you are in the middle of a situation; but, a lot of the things that fall into this category could be avoided, so I'm less sympathetic when someone divorces for this reason, especially when there are women out there who really are suffering and have very legitimate reasons for needing to get out of marriage.

OUR LIPS ARE SEALED

He just won't freakin' talk to you! It's so frustrating. Your dog can communicate his needs better. Men are notoriously bad communicators when it comes to relationships. But, honestly, that is a widely perpetuated myth that doesn't have to be the case. Everyone has to work at communication, and just because women are willing to talk more, it doesn't mean they are actually communicating effectively. If you find this is an area of your relationship that is lacking, there are a number of things you can do to fix it, as I covered in Phase 1.

If you and your partner just can't get on the same page, no matter how hard you try, you may decide that divorce is your best option. But, I need to warn you, divorcing is not going to solve your communication problems. In fact, it is highly likely to make them worse; so, even if you decide to go ahead with divorce, you should not give up on trying to improve your communication with your soon-to-be ex. Otherwise you are in for a really bumpy ride.

THE NEW THING

This is another area where I think a lot of heartache and wasted years could be avoided if you'd just taken the time to ask the right questions and get to know the person early on. What were their goals in life? Is it always a new thing, or can they be satisfied with what they have. But, there are also situations where people grow in different directions, opportunities arise that change ambitions, and life circumstances alter how you look at things.

Maybe you thought you wanted kids at the start, but now your career is thriving in ways you never imagined and you've decided that's a bigger priority and where you want to focus your energy. Maybe your husband realized as he's gotten older that his faith is more important to him than it was when he was younger, but you don't share that faith. (We'll touch on religious/cultural differences in greater detail later, but this is an area that can cause a lot of strife.) It could be that you need to move closer to family to care for ailing parents and he doesn't have as many opportunities in that area. You can try to anticipate changes like this and discuss them, but life is going to throw you curve balls. If the goals are different enough and important enough, it can be a reason people choose to split. Hopefully there are no kids in the mix, or else you should exhaust every effort to find a compromise that works for everyone. This should not create a lot of strife in your divorce unless you let resentments over the fact that things changed affect how you deal with each other.

MONY MONY

The issues around mony mony and financial burdens are at the top of the reasons marriages fall apart for a good reason—it's stressful! Your ex is not going to be making you feel so good, or so fine and you will not say yeah, yeah, yeah when he's going out of his way to be unfair in the divorce. Whether you're single or trying to support a family, when money gets tight, so does the ability you have to be flexible and take things in stride. You become short-tempered and panicked. But, it's not just the strain of struggling to pay the bills that brings tension into a marriage. Even if you have plenty of mony mony, how you spend it can also create difficult feelings. Maybe you over-spend to compensate for the fact that you aren't getting the attention and emotional support you need in a marriage (a.k.a. retail therapy). Or, it could be that he holds the purse strings too tightly and you feel like you're being treated like a child. Maybe he's really secretive about all of your finances and you begin to grow suspicious. All of those things lead to distrust in your marriage.

Don't expect that to change if you are going through a divorce. In fact, count on them getting even worse and bringing up fears, doubts, and insecurities you had never considered. Money is tricky business and people attach a lot of emotion to it. While it is important to make sure your needs and your children's needs are going to be met when you are settling your divorce, don't let fear of not having enough create a contentious situation that will escalate into a long drawn out divorce that really only results in the lawyers having most of that money you were fighting over. But, if your ex is Cray-Cray (a.k.a. a narcissist) and needs to see you suffer, unfortunately you will be going to court, all your money fears are probably legitimate, and you will most likely lose most of what you have.

I RAN

Well, there's not a lot you can do if he ran so far away. If your husband bails on you, it is going to be painful and scary and confusing. You will question yourself and your perception of the life you built together. You will second-guess every time he ever said he loved you and all the promises he made. Flower, if you are going through this. All I can say is that I'm sorry. But, you also should not spend a single second wishing to get him back.

Getting through your divorce with dignity and self-respect is your best hope because remembering that you are a woman of value and don't deserve such treatment is the best way to make him regret his decision, show your children that you will survive, and move on to find someone who will recognize and cherish all you have to offer. Just because he stole away into the night and out of your life doesn't mean he gets to steal your self-worth and your future.

WANNA BE STARTING SOMETHING

In different ways, emotional abuse is worse than physical abuse because it slowly eats away at your self-worth. It can cause some major psychological scars that will be with you for life. Constant criticism, intimidation, shaming, manipulation, controlling, etc. Most men who abuse were hurt as a child and didn't learn healthy coping methods. I know a lot of women who love to fix men, but this type of man can't be fixed by you; they need professional help. He must really want to change, and for all of you who know a man like this, you know that's not going to happen. They most likely have some major personality disorder, and the recovery rate is really low. You really need to leave or you will end up sick and full of anxiety.

There is nothing you could possible do to deserve this kind of treatment; there is nothing you can possibly do to change him; and there is nothing in the world that would make sticking around a good idea. I will warn you, precious Flower, divorces from abusive men are really tricky and scary. My guess is that part of why you stayed as long as you did was to avoid what you think may happen (and you're probably only scratching the surface with what you imagine). But, that doesn't mean you should stay. Find a safe place, ask for help from someone who is equipped to help you, know your options, and act quickly. There are many resources out there for women in your situation and lots of people eager to help you get out.

JESSIE'S GIRL

Is your husband having Jessie's girl? Or, does he just wish that he had her? If you find yourself even entertaining the question, "Is my spouse cheating," odds are good that they are. I know that is not what you want to hear; but, I believe most people instinctively know that their spouse is having an affair, though you may choose to ignore the signs. I don't think anyone is purposely out there "affairing" it up to hurt their spouse or children. They're in denial . . . and lust. I could fill this entire book just talking about the range of emotions that come from infidelity and the fallout of it, but let's just summarize it by saying it doesn't feel good and the effects are long-lasting.

Some people choose to stay in a marriage after the spouse has been caught cheating and I think that is a very personal and individual decision. I think the only reason you should consider it is if your spouse has come clean on their own and bent over backward to make amends, but you have to assess your personal situation for yourself. You should be aware that whether you choose to stay or head to the lawyer, the worst thing you can do is allow their betrayal to affect your sense of self-worth. That's all on him!

WHITE LINES

Get higher baby, higher baby. Addiction is tricky and sometimes they don't ever come down. Sometimes you get signs early on, and sometimes it doesn't manifest until later in life and you may already be really invested. It is a disease that can bring pain and problems of all sorts into your marriage. In fact, nearly every reason for divorce that we've listed could be triggered by an active addiction—different goals/priorities, financial problems, adultery, abuse.

Discovering your partner has an addiction does not automatically mean divorce. If they are willing to get help and do the work necessary and stay in a program that offers them ongoing support for this thing that will be with them for a lifetime, and you also get the help you need to know the right way to support them, then you can work to save your relationship. But, if they are not willing to get help or even to admit they have a problem, you really only have two choices: accept the daily hell you are inviting into your world and just live with it or get a divorce. It might feel like you are abandoning someone who is unhealthy and needs support, but if they are not willing to do anything to help themselves, the only thing you are doing by staying is enabling them.

Whatever your reasons for divorce, understand that there are going to be a full range of emotions that everyone involved will experience, and they will come up unexpectedly (often at inopportune times). The best you can do is recognize that all of them are normal and try to keep yourself focused on the priority, which is making sure you honor yourself in the process and protect your children from as much fallout as possible.

PART-TIME LOVER

Isn't anyone worried about STD's besides me? You and me, He and She, She and She, He and He are part-time lovers. And that's withoug my going to get into all the people I know who are in throuples (polyamory). I even knew swingers when I lived in conservative Maryland. I personally don't know how you could be having sex with another person while you're married, but people do it. Look at Denis Clarke, he's got a whole family on the side! Let's go into a little history here.

The first recorded case of divorce, according to History.com, was that of Anne Clarke in 1643. The grounds for divorce were that Denis Clarke abandoned his wife and two kids to be with another woman. He admitted in a signed affidavit, to having done just that. He had two children with his mistress as well and refused to go back to his wife.

Divorces were much more difficult to get up until the last fifty years, but adultery and abandonment were (and, sadly, still are) certainly a sure way to get one granted.[2] And, just because there are many who have gone before you and many who will, unfortunately, come after you, it doesn't make the process any easier or less of an emotional upheaval. Even divorces that happen amicably carry with them some sense of sadness and failure that the parties have to deal with.

Maybe you see yourself in one of these scenarios. Maybe your divorce is driven by something unique. The reasons are less important than being prepared for what is coming and equipping yourself for making informed choices that will protect you and your children. That starts by being in the right headspace. Let's talk about what that means.

I GET SO EMOTIONAL
Get ready, pretty, Flower! You can get emotional when you think of him. Just, remember, marriage is love, divorce is business, and no two divorces are alike. Even if you could find a parallel universe scenario where the couples were the same age, same personality types, came from the same socio-economic and religious backgrounds, had the same amount of stuff and assets to divide, and the same number of kids and pets, and they are divorcing for the same reasons, you're still going to have two totally different outcomes because people react differently to the stressors that come from this emotionally-charged ordeal. Sometimes even one individual will respond differently from one minute to the next depending on what's going on with them, and how cray-cray they are at the time. Ain't it shocking what love can do?

The thing is, some of what you are feeling isn't as simple as the surface emotion you identify. You could be getting turned on and knocked off your feet at the same

2   http://www.history.com/this-day-in-history/first-divorce-in-the-colonies

time. There can be lots of things wrapped up in one feeling. For example, you might think you are just trying to protect yourself when really it's your need for control creeping in and taking over. It's normal to get so emotional, baby when you think of your soon-to-be-ex and what you won't have with them any longer and what they might be doing now that they are gone. Even if you are the one who wanted the divorce, you may find yourself second-guessing your decision at times. We're going to look at the most common emotions that are likely to come up in divorce so you will at least have some idea of what to expect and won't wonder if you've lost your mind when you feel like you are experiencing some sort of Jekyll and Hyde transformation.

DON'T FORGET MY NUMBER

Yes, in an ideal world your split from your husband is a matter of two mature people agreeing that they just don't belong together and they are better off living separately. You may want to try to stay on good terms with your ex, divide up your stuff equitably, and part as friends. Maybe you even save each other's numbers as your emergency contacts. (Are you laughing yet? Because this is where things are funny.). As much as you might like to stay friends with your ex—and I'm not saying you can't—it isn't going to happen right away. You need distance to get through all of the hard parts of divorce and trying to maintain a relationship with them just muddies the waters.

Note: What I'm talking about is different from being civil and respectful with one another during a divorce. You can and should do that. I'm talking about still having them over to the house for dinner, allowing them to stay the night so they can help get the kids off to school in the morning, calling them anytime anything goes wrong. If you are divorcing, he is not your person any longer, and treating him that way is bound to end up creating confusion. You're better off taking the time apart you need to adjust to the new normal of not sharing everything, and then, after the divorce is final, gradually making room for them in your life in a different way.

EVERY BREATH YOU TAKE

If you don't listen to any other advice I give you, please at least heed this bit. Stay off of social media during your divorce. I'm going to explain some of the legal reasons in the next chapter, but here and now I'm telling you not to torture yourself by trolling your soon-to-be-ex on Facebook or Instagram. At best, you are distracting yourself from other things that need to be your focus—taking care of your kids, doing self-care, finding new passions or career opportunities—and at worst you are going to find information you do not want to have or that may be misleading and send you down a rabbit hole that will not end well.

Declare a moratorium on social media activity until you are on the other side of your divorce for your own well-being. Give yourself space and distance in the virtual world as well as the real world for as long as you are sorting through all of the crazy emotions and impulses that are bound to come up. You'll be glad you did when you don't have to see your ex looking happy at a party and when you don't have to deal with all of your well-meaning friends and family (or his snarky friends and family) asking how you are doing and if they can do anything to help. Just spare yourself that headache. You'll thank me later.

HARD TO SAY I'M SORRY

You're probably going to think I've betrayed you when I tell you that you need to apologize to your ex, but you do. Saying "I'm Sorry" might be one of the hardest things you have to do, but if you really want closure, this is part of it.

GOODBYE TO YOU

With very few exceptions, we all bear some responsibility in the deterioration of the relationship. Yes, your husband may be 99.99% responsible for things falling apart, but by owning your part in the divorce, being honest with yourself about things you could have done better, how you could have handled responses more effectively, or ways you could have deescalated a situation or offered more support are all part of healing and preparing yourself for moving on.

And you know what else? There is so much power in apologizing to him and owning your shit, you won't believe how it feels after you do it. You're probably thinking, *Annette, saying I did something wrong gives him the upper hand.* But, the truth is, he won't see it coming and it will take him completely off his game. You also get the satisfaction of knowing you took the high road, so do this for yourself as you are sorting through all of the feelings. I asked you to do an honest personal inventory before deciding to divorce, so look at those things and think about what you can apologize for and then release it and grow from it. It will make you an even more beautiful Flower when you can release all of that toxicity.

LOST IN EMOTION

Don't call me melodramatic when I say you may feel like you're dying. You may get lost in the emotions you are experiencing because you don't understand that the pain you feel from the ending of a marriage is very similar to what you would experience in a loss through death.

Everyone is familiar with the five stages of grief that Elisabeth Kubler-Ross describes in her book Death and Dying. But what a lot of people don't realize is that divorce holds its own kind of grief. The only difference is that with divorce you still have to see the person while dealing with the loss of your connection to them. It's almost like being haunted by the person you lost, but not in a *Poltergeist* type of way. You still have to interact with your ex, and it's hard to obtain the closure you need when they are still in your life, but in a way that makes them feel like a stranger. It's a trauma that keeps repeating itself. The ex just keeps showing up to show you they aren't dead at all, they are very well alive and you are going to have to deal with them for a long, long time if you have children together.

The death of a spouse is its own unique kind of hell and I'm not trying to diminish it. I'm just saying that the grief that comes from a divorce, no matter how amicable it might be, is just as valid and requires time to heal, but nobody gives you bereavement time to do so. We are going to look at the five stages in the context of divorce to help you recognize these feelings when they arise and know what the hell to do with them.

WHERE DO BROKEN HEARTS GO

Now that we've talked about the most common reasons for divorce and we should probably talk about the likely stages of processing those feelings. Not only will you wonder where your broken heart can go for healing, but you may wonder where your rational mind went as well! There are a lot of unreasonable thoughts and desires that will come up as a part of sorting through the rubble of your marriage. Some are helpful, but others can be really destructive. The choices you make during this time of transition are going to have a lasting impact on everyone, so proceed with caution.

SUDDENLY

Some wake up suddenly and they are in love, others stay asleep and they are way deep in denial, there is no beauty up above, only the hell of not being able to move forward. The "Powers that Be" gave us the greatest gift to help us maintain our sanity when our realities are just too horrible for us to face: denial. Being able to retreat to a safe place where you aren't being directly confronted with the pain of your loss is perfectly normal and probably necessary for a time. When your system is in a fragile state, the harsh light of reality can be too much to handle. A little bit of denial until you can have a minute to lick your wounds can help you face your situation with a stronger frame of mind.

But this is a temporary fix. Staying in denial is the greatest obstacle to healing; you simply can't fix something until you identify what it is and come up with a solution. Denial prevents you from being able to identify what is wrong. Staying in denial ends up manifesting in a lot of unhealthy ways:

1.   we make excuses;
2.   we ignore the truth;
3.   we pretend it isn't happening;
4.   we blame other people;
5.   we may even blame ourselves.

Denial is the first phase of grief because, bottom line, the truth fucking hurts and accepting that your marriage is over (whether you chose to end it because you couldn't live with what your relationship had become or he did by walking away) is going to be really hard and take time.

Denial is a tricky bastard to overcome. You're not fighting your ex here; you're essentially fighting yourself. You're fighting to stay in the safe world you created where you didn't have to face the truth you stuffed way down inside the deep dark place within yourself. What's even more likely is that you've been in denial for much of your marriage and have ignored the red flags that were letting you know something was wrong.

It's okay to ease yourself into facing what's staring you in the face, but eventually you will have to come out of hiding. Try doing this incrementally, taking one aspect of your situation at a time and figure out how to put it in its proper perspective. Or you might do better if you try to treat it like you are listening to a stranger share their story. Being able to look at something from an objective, outsider's view could allow you to be less emotionally attached to the circumstances. But, trust me, Flower, if you stay where you are, you are only going to make things worse and your kids will suffer too. The upside is that with each piece you put into place, the more strength you find to look at the whole picture head on. Life is a journey; become a good friend to yourself so when things come and go in your life you will know you have someone you can trust to lean on and get you through!

SLEDGEHAMMER
Anger is a completely normal, usually healthy, human emotion. Anger is a complicated emotion, to be sure, and sometimes it's not easy to parse out all of the things that are triggering it. But, unless we understand the suffering that underlies our anger, it will fester and erupt in unproductive ways.

We may believe that others cause our anger; but, really, anger lies within us. There is usually some inner wound that, when touched by an external influence—a stranger's harsh or unkind words, your friend's lack of availability, your husband's insensitivity—flares up and results in an expression of anger. Being able to acknowledge what's at the root of the emotion, realizing that you may be lashing out at the wrong person, gaining insight into the trigger, and releasing your anger in a healthy way will help you begin healing as you go through a divorce.

Anger is a necessary part of the healing process when it is expressed in a way that isn't destructive. For some people, writing a letter to your ex, pouring out all of the things you wish you could say to his face but are too emotional to express might be useful . . . But, don't send it!! This is just for you so you can sort through all of the things that are feeding your anger. I wouldn't be able to do this because I can't resist sharing what I write—I can't not hit the *fuck you* button (commonly known as the *SEND* button)—but it could be very cathartic for you. Another option is to take up kickboxing or get a punching bag to physically release the toxic emotions welling up inside you. Just don't take a sledgehammer to any of his possessions, or at least be a smart Flower and don't get caught doing it. But, I would really recommend meditation, yoga, and massage as better options. Whatever it takes to work through the anger, do that for yourself because letting it build up until you can't hold it in any longer is not healthy, especially since the odds are really good that the person who is the source of your pain isn't going to bear the brunt of your outburst.

WISHING WELL

Slowly, surely, sweetly, softly, quickly, loudly. This is probably the most pathetic phase of grief because it's when we really lower our standards and convince ourselves that settling for something less than what we really want will make us happy. When a loved one dies, we may tell God we will do A, B, or C if only we could have just a few more minutes with them or if he would just send them back. Obviously, that is beyond unrealistic, but people ask for crazy things out of desperation.

I've seen women bargaining with their ex to try to stay together because they don't want to be alone or don't have an education and are afraid of trying to support themselves and the kids without him. I get the impulse to try everything possible to stop the pain and nightmare of a divorce, but you're really just delaying the inevitable. Staying in a marriage with someone who treats you badly and doesn't respect your vows is not going to end well, and hanging on and begging him to stay will only weaken you, cause you to lose his respect, and increase the likelihood of even more pain to come.

When you find yourself in the bargaining stage, try sitting down with a pad of paper and writing out all the traits you look for in a partner. Try to remember what you dreamed your life would be like once you found the perfect man. Write those things in a column and then do an honest inventory of how many of those things you have right now in the spouse and the marriage you are trying to hold onto. Now, remember you have to be realistic about your expectations. If one of your ideals was a tall, dark, handsome man with vaults full of cash and your husband is short, moderately attractive, and makes an average living, maybe you do need to re-evaluate your priorities and give him another shot. But, if you expected to have a husband who was kind and loyal and your guy is disrespectful in the way he talks to you and treats you, then, Flower, what is it that is so appealing to you? The sex? Because let me tell you, a good vibrator will get you there just as well and without all the blows to your self-esteem.

Bargaining is what we do when we think we can't accept what is happening to us. Looking at your situation without the rose-colored glasses will help you see that what you have may not really be a bargain and what's on the other side of the divorce could be the deal of a lifetime.

SAD SONGS (SAY SO MUCH)

As we move through the stages of grief and get past the parts that are designed to keep us from feeling, we hit the one where we feel *everything* and it can lead to a little depression. It usually hits us square in the face out of nowhere and we collapse under the weight of the pain. The day you realize that all of this really is happening and you come to the clarity of everything you've lost, you will mourn deeply and in places you didn't know could feel pain. When it finally hit me, I mourned the loss of my family as well as my dream of the perfect family. I mourned the loss of the life we built together, the future we dreamed of, but would never have. I mourned the loss of the security of having someone to back me up, the comfort of sharing the gifts and the hardships of life, the sense of belonging in being part of a family. Little by little, I began to discover all of the things that were going with him out the door, and my foundation crumbled.

Grief, at this stage, can hang over us like a wet wool blanket and it can be smothering. It is an important part of the process, but it is one that can consume you if you aren't careful. Allow yourself to feel all the feels. Let yourself do the ugly cry until your tears are dried up. Lie in bed and eat shitty junk food for a week. Wear your pajamas everywhere, and don't brush your hair if that's what you need to do. (Please just brush your teeth.) Give yourself this time to just wallow in it, but set a time limit for how long you are going to indulge yourself. You'll have to decide for yourself how long you need; although, I will say that if, after a month, you are still in your PJs, barely getting your kids to school on time with a sack lunch of only Skittles and Cheetos, you're probably pushing it a bit far and need to go take a shower and pull yourself together.

One of the great things about my Beverly Hills Eulogy Parties is that they not only give women the opportunity to mourn in front of their friends and family, they give themselves permission to do so (and in a pretty fabulous way), and after that comes healing. Be sad because it's okay that you are, but be ready to find your joy as well.

NEW SENSATION

Eventually, you will accept that you're getting divorced or are divorced. The new sensation you feel might not just be the vibrator your gay BFF got you so you'd stop being so cranky through your divorce. You'll begin to see that life is good and you need to start enjoying it. You may still be a bit angry or a bit depressed, but you won't be wishing that your ex gets hit by a UPS truck. Once you are in this place you will be able to see clearly why it ended and that it had to end. Hopefully you have learned a lot about yourself and grown out of it because that's what really helps you accept and move on.

Acceptance isn't one of those things I can really help you through with tips and suggestions for how to make it go more smoothly. It's something you have to come to on your own. But, if you take a little of the advice I've offered for the other stages, odds are good you will arrive at this stage sooner than you expect and will be more than ready to step into a new phase of life.

SHOUT, SHOUT

Let it ALL out. I believe in expressing yourself loudly, perhaps because I'm part Italian. You may do this with a close friend or family member. You may want to do this with a therapist. Regardless of who you vent to, it is important to process everything that has happened, what fears you have, how you might have changed things, how you want to move forward, and every other thought and emotion that arises. Pretending you don't feel a certain way is not going to stop that feeling from happening, and usually it chooses to rear its ugly head at the most inopportune moments.

I hear there is actually shouting therapy that is very productive. There's something cleansing about yelling at the top of your lungs about how unfair you think something is or how mad you are or how stupid you feel. Just get it all out because, once you do, then you get to do the work of unpacking all of those unpleasant and destructive messages you've been holding onto and you can replace them with new, positive, healing ones instead. Purging all of the negativity that comes up in a divorce and all of the problems that led up to it in the first place is a really important piece of self-care that is going to help you move forward.

GOODBYE TO YOU

PAIN AND SUFFERING

Pain and Suffering. Hopefully it isn't as dark as Iggy Pop painted it; but, I've read numerous articles on the subject of grief, and my conclusion is that men and women suffer equally after a breakup. There are just gender differences in how grief is expressed. Women suffer openly. We don't stuff our feelings the way men do, and it can be disconcerting when we don't see the signs of his suffering too! We want to see their pain for reassurance that they are feeling the loss too—some sign that this mattered and losing us wasn't easy. You may not get to see your ex in all of his tear-streaked, bathrobe-wearing, ice-cream binging glory, but you can rest assured he is going through his own stages of grief.

Remember, as women, we tend to take a healthier approach to grief because we can. Men are conditioned from a very young age to shove aside these types of feelings and not risk this kind of vulnerability. We have the luxury of being able to call any friend and tell them we are going through a break-up and they will talk to us for hours in the middle of the night and give us the emotional support we need. Unfortunately, men rarely receive the same support. Grief looks different for everyone, but no one is immune to it when it comes to the loss that is part of divorce. Give yourself time, be gentle with yourself, and trust that your heart will heal if you treat it well.

FREEDOM

I really am sorry you are going through all of this, but you are on your way to freedom. Whether you wanted the divorce or the divorce was not your choosing, you will still be free— free from a person you no longer want to be married to or free from someone who doesn't want to be married to you who you shouldn't want to be with anymore. I hope my 80s humor is keeping you laughing. If not, I hope it gives you a little smile every now and then. Hell, I'll even take a smirk. Just do what you can to stay happy and positive so you can attract more happy and positive things. I know, I know, easier said than done when the shit is hitting the fan. Let's move on and get you through the tough section that none of us ever dreamed we would face. You will get through it and come out stronger, I promise.

Chapter 5
WILD, WILD WEST

North, East, West, South, you don't know where the hell you are heading, but it's definitely not to the same house. The world of divorce with its attorneys and courtrooms and documents will make you feel like you're in the wild, wild west. Your ex is going to be mean and he doesn't care, as long as he doesn't have to give you money.

Even if you've never been in a courtroom I'm sure you've seen enough legal dramas on TV to have some picture in your head about what you might experience. Let me settle one thing for you right now. It may feel like your divorce is drama-packed enough to be one of their storylines, but reality plays out a lot more slowly and will not be wrapped up in one hour. Plus, remember it may not be your ex who's dragging out the divorce, it could be his lawyer who wants to make the most money out of his anger. He's all on board trying to bring you to your knees and doesn't care at what cost if he has the money to do so.

I can't promise you your divorce will not turn into a showdown; but, if you follow the advice I'm offering, I can assure you that you will be as prepared as you possibly can be and you will be better equipped for avoiding some of the traps that people often encounter.

THE COWBOY RIDES AWAY

You are feeling awful right now, maybe you're drinking too much and eating way too much, or maybe you can't even eat at all. You feel this weird combo of shitty and sad at the same time. Divorce is taking a toll on you, and now I'm going to tell you in the midst of your turmoil, that your cowboy road away a long time ago!

Darling Flowers, I hate to tell you, we all got super gypped! Do you know what we missed out on? In the first half of the 20th century, people thought divorce was inappropriate, and admitting you were getting divorced was scandalous. Most states intentionally dragged out divorces in the hopes that the delays and suffering you were going to endure would make you reconsider—well, everywhere except Nevada. Nevada was a poor state and looked at divorce as a source of income for the state. As long as you'd been a resident of Nevada for six months, you could walk into a courthouse in your fancy shoes and walk out divorced.

In 1931, the Nevada legislature got even smarter. They shortened the residency period to six weeks and made it financially affordable for the average person to get divorced. And someone even had the brain child to create "Divorce Ranches" that were like adult summer camps where you could swim and ride horses with handsome cowboys while establishing your residency to get your divorce![3]

But, just as with summer camp, eventually it comes to an end and real life takes over. When the other states in the union finally accepted the reality that people were getting divorced anyway, and there was money to be made in it, the Divorce Ranches were put out of business. But, sadly, the business of divorce did not die out with the Ranches; we just found a different way to turn it into an industry—an industry without any fun and that mostly benefits lawyers.

So, now we have to suffer in this day and age. I don't know where all the cowboys have gone, but they aren't helping us through our divorces anymore. Although, I did spend so much time at the courthouse that I met a very handsome young lawyer. We just would've had more fun riding horses or swimming than having coffee in the courthouse cafeteria. Though you may feel like you missed the stagecoach on

3   https://timeline.com/reno-divorce-ranches-cowboys-c0539fa085b6

this easier way through, life has a way of turning bad into good. Remember, Charlotte from *Sex in the City* married her divorce lawyer. You never know who you are going to meet who might be a new love interest or at least become a good friend you can call for legal advice.

FIGHT FIRE WITH FIRE

The reason the first chapter in this phase focused on dealing with the emotions that come up in divorce is that until you can let go of your emotionally charged feelings around it, you will not be mentally prepared to handle the legal aspects of it.

Angry, depressed, scared, lonely people going through divorce don't think of the stress they create for their families. It's very difficult to take care of yourself, let alone your children, when you haven't resolved the negative feelings you're experiencing. When your emotions are running amok it's going to feel like you're fighting a blazing wild fire with a squirt gun, and if you are in the midst of an ugly court battle you will wonder where all of the law and order went. But, here's the reality: If you think your divorce is going to come off without a hitch, think again. Depending on how much you spend on lawyers, who's willing to play dirty, and how much stamina you have, it can turn into a real showdown.

Let me offer you a Divorce 101 that will help you fight fire with fire.

1. *Consult an attorney.* You must be completely informed about you rights and responsibilities.
2. *Put together documents.* Go through all your tax returns, investment statements, bank statements, life insurance policies, mortgage information, credit card statements, wills, social security statements, etc. Your attorney will need all of this.
3. *List expenses and make a budget.* Do you know all of your

monthly expenses? You will need to have all of this in detail so your attorney can calculate a realistic demand for support.

4. *Record possessions.* You are going to need to list the furniture, artwork, jewelry, cars, and appliances so the court can value your tangible assets.

5. *Itemize debt.* Flower, let's hope you're not in debt. If you are, you should consider getting rid of it before you get divorced. This can cause some issues during the divorce.

6. *Document your income.* I hope you earn a lot! But, it you've been a stay-at-home mom for a while, you need to figure out your employability. I hope you went back to school like I suggested in the second chapter.

7. *Document his income.* This is pretty straight forward if he earns a regular salary. You have his pay stubs. If he's self-employed it gets a little tricky, so try to see if you can track the money coming in over the last year or so.

8. *Get a nest egg.* Don't ever get divorced without having a little money stashed away somewhere. If he's vindictive and cuts you off, how will you buy milk for your children? Start saving before you talk about divorce. Make a plan.

9. *Fix your credit.* Having a good credit rating can make or break you. If you don't have credit cards in your own name, you need to go out there and get a few. You may have to get an apartment, and if you have bad credit or no credit rating of your own, that will be difficult. You don't want to go and live with your mom if you don't have to, which could be worse than staying with your husband for some women.

10. *Look out for your fabulous children.* Make your children your number one priority right now. I know it's hard

when you are going through hell and need free time to heal, cry, and think. But, they are going through hell too.

PAPER IN FIRE

You're hurt and confused, but you have to make decisions that will affect your financial future. Don't fuck this up because you're upset that he's not taking the kids so he can go horseback riding with his new twenty-one-year-old girlfriend with a very large tongue ring. I'm not a financial planner, but these are things you need to be aware of and get professional advice on.

1. *Future Security* - Don't just focus on your alimony; you must look to the future and hire a financial planner if you have a lot of money. Don't sign anything without doing this!

2. *QDRO* - Yes, those are four letters that you won't know unless you are divorced. It means Qualified Domestic Relations Order. It's a legal document that tells how you decided to divide the contribution plan. You can lose important pension rights if you don't have a QDRO in place. The administrator of the plan can't give you the payments without this.

3. *Investments* - Get a professional opinion if you think that you are settling for investments that will or won't grow over the years. He may want you to take some stock instead of the cash. This can be super risky! That investment might not work out and you could've taken the cash, which always works out.

4. *Pension Plans* - A defined benefit plan (DBP) is a pension plan. It's controlled and funded by the employer. You are entitled to the share of its value as of today. Here you may need to hire an actuary. An actuary is a specially trained financial expert to calculate the value of the DBP.

5. *Debt* - If you are leaving your husband because of his gambling problem, you may have a lot of debt, and unfortunately, you owe half. If the debt was incurred during your marriage, it's a shared liability. The credit card companies will be coming after you in the future.

6. *Child Support and Alimony* - You must request that your spouse obtain life and disability insurance policies to ensure that you will get paid if your spouse becomes disabled or dies. Your spouse can decide to stop paying at any time and these policies won't help you in that case. But, you can go back to court and the judge will not be happy about it.

7. *Expenses* – I know I mentioned this in the previous section, and we all hate doing these things, but it's mandatory. Do you know down to the penny where your money goes each month? You have to write down all of your expenses and make a budget. When you write these things down to the penny you may get a big reality check of what lifestyle you will be living in the future.

8. *Home* - You don't want to get in over your head here. I know it's probably best to keep the kids in their home and school district, and your ex should want to help you with that for his children, but that's not usually the case. If you do keep your house, just make sure you made a budget that is realistic and you can cover the mortgage and all those little owning-a-home-expenses that come up.

THE DEVIL'S RIGHT HAND

In the divorce world, the term "Narcissist" comes up all the time. Again, I'm not going to diagnose another human's mental problems because I'm not qualified, but I don't need a medical degree to diagnose your ex as cray-cray if he keeps trying to take you to court to hurt you, especially if you have his kids most of the time. There really isn't a reason to go to court. Most things can be settled through mediation, so if your ex needs the judge to make all the rulings and wants to throw you under the bus publicly, then I'm going to call it: he is cray-cray . . . and a terrible business man because the cost is not smart. He's probably also easily influenced by his attorney who's probably throwing logs on the fire so they can make more money off his anger. Your ex's new girlfriend/ wife may be putting pressure on him to make sure you aren't going to get one dime that he can spend on her. If she is in the googly-eyed, blindness of new love, she won't care if you have kids to take care of and he cheated or abused you, and wouldn't believe he did those things even if Jesus came down from Heaven and told her that was the truth. Everyone thinks these cray-cray men are smart, but they're not. Intelligent people know they have to eventually settle and they should do it quickly to avoid the costs. As the saying goes, "Don't cut your nose off to spite your face."

If you are divorcing someone who thinks he is so damned important that the world will end without him, who is so freaking special that he needs constant attention, who lacks empathy and is an overall arrogant prick, then you are really screwed during your divorce. The best thing to do here is figure out why you married someone like this, grow, and never do it again. Take responsibility and get a lot of therapy. And stay single for a while so you don't risk attracting another cray-cray person. Enjoy these stories about cray-cray men. If you are divorcing a good man, please count your blessings because what I am sharing here is what so many women go through.

SAY HELLO TO RONNIE

Ronnie was hiding his money from his ex everywhere he possibly could. A court order was enforced for him to show his ex his tax returns every year because he would quit jobs or take a leave of absence and then take her back to court between very high paying jobs for a re-evaluation of support. He refused to provide his tax return each year because he felt it was a violation of his privacy. At the same time, Ronnie would subpoena his ex-wife's bank statements to see how she was spending "his" money.

MAJOR TOM

Major Tom might be a major, but he is also a major prick. Poor Jenny actually caught her husband having sex with someone at a motel and he told the court that she didn't see what she saw. She must have looked in the wrong window at the motel. He claimed that when she pounded on the door, he didn't want to open let her in because he was on the phone with his mother, which seems suspicious since he was able to use the phone to call the police on her to get her to leave. (This was years ago, before people had cell phones.) The police came and told her to leave. She had their children with her who had to witness this scene. The judge saw through his version of events and granted the divorce based on infidelity rather than the irreconcilable differences he claimed.

GLORIA

Gloria's ex told everyone she was crazy because she saw a psychiatrist. He found out this information because his office was around the corner from their house and her friend saw the same doctor. She was being abused emotionally and he was cheating on her during the marriage. He had a drinking problem and had his driver's license revoked. He even made her get up at 4:00 am to drive him to work in the snow right after having a baby. During the divorce he tried to get the kids taken away and told everyone that she was crazy because she took a small dose of an anti-anxiety medication called Paxil.

I can give these examples all day, but I'll stop here.

CHAPTER 5

If you are divorcing a cray-cray man and think he is going to follow the divorce agreement, you are in *Twilight Zone*. You can spend thousands of dollars on court enforcements and he's still not going to follow it. He knows if he doesn't, nothing really happens. It's really hard going to court; it's so much time and money. If you're not rich, it's hard to take time off from work and hire a lawyer to enforce something that someone doesn't want to do or pay. The court will give you some money if he makes more than you, but there will still be a few months' salary gone and your kids will suffer. Be prepared for cray-cray behavior during your divorce, and keep yourself safe.

Now, let's talk about the good guys! Maybe your husband is decent and things just didn't work out. He doesn't want you or the kids to suffer just because you both fell out of love. If you are divorcing a good man and he is doing the right thing for you and your kids, you are very lucky and should try to be kind and loving to him. Do extra for him and he will do extra for you, and your kids will grow up in a great two-parent lifestyle that's full of love.

AXEL F

Axel F did cheat, and I think he's a prick for cheating on his wife when he had two beautiful little girls at home. I'm not saying he's the good guy in the marriage and his Karma will get him, but I'm saying he was the good guy in the divorce. He left his wife for his mistress, but he gave his wife the house so his children didn't have to suffer and change schools. He made sure his ex-wife was financially taken care of. He didn't want their world to change a lot because of his wrongdoings. I have to give him a shout out for admitting the affair and taking care of his family. It's rare that a man will cop to his mistakes and do the right thing for his family. Most cheaters don't come clean about affairs, which makes them liars too, and liars don't usually don't do the right thing.

JIMMIE DEAN

Jimmie Dean's wife left him. He did not want the divorce and was heartbroken. He was the kind of good guy all women say they want. He took the higher road and insisted on mediation to keep the costs down, and asked her for a lot of the custody. He was the good dad who spent as much time as he could with his kids. During the divorce he got some amazing job offers out of state, but he's not the type of man who would miss five minutes of his visitation with the kids, or even a school performance. I knew a guy who made 1.4 million per year but told his ex-wife he didn't have enough money to go to his son's middle school graduation since he lived out of state. Why women leave the good guy with his priorities in order is beyond me, but I'm not here to judge anyone. I don't know what path you belong on.

HANGIN' TOUGH

Divorce sucks and there is no way around it. It doesn't matter if it's nothing more than a mistake you made during a drunken Vegas weekend, you're going to have to deal with some legalities to get it done. The best you can hope for is that there is no video proof of your poor choices (unlike certain boy bands who are still trying to live down the 80s) and that your soon-to-be ex also wants to get it over as quickly as you do. But, in most cases, you are dissolving a relationship that consumed much of your adult life, and it's going to be painful and complicated, and you will have to hang tough to come out of the ordeal without deep wounds and mountains of debt.

I'm going to lay out some really important factors to consider as you are preparing to dive into the legal part of your divorce. Please keep these things in mind so you can avoid a lot of the headaches and nightmares.

COLD-HEARTED SNAKE

Yeah, look into his eyes, he's probably going to tell you some lies so he can take your money. We've all heard at least one joke about how soul-less and greedy lawyers are. And, it's true, there are a lot of cold-hearted snakes lying in wait in the tall grass. There are ethical, good attorneys out there, but you have to do your due diligence and get recommendations, check up on them, and interview them before committing. The internet is your friend here. Thanks to the technology we have available, you can find out what you need to know about the person representing you and your interests as long as you take the time to look.

Attorneys aren't cheap, no matter who you hire, so be prepared to spend a lot of money; but, you should also know that trying to bargain hunt when it comes to the person who is going to guide you through the legal process of dissolving your marriage could cost you more in the long run. This is one area where the old saying, "You get what you pay for," applies most of the time. Sure, there are some high-priced lawyers who charge a whole lot for doing very little; but, usually, what you are paying for is someone who has a lot of experience and a good track record with their clients. In addition to making sure your attorney got a good education and has had good success in court, you want to make sure you are selecting the right type of counsel for your needs. It's just like with doctors. If you need brain surgery, you don't go to a podiatrist. And, if you need a divorce and have custody issues to resolve, (even though you may feel like your ex is a miscreant) you don't want to hire a criminal defense attorney. They know the anatomy of the law, but their specialty—the area where they have focused their knowledge—requires a different approach.

The bottom line is you need to have confidence in your attorney—in their ability to get the job done for you and in their ability to see you as a real person with real concerns, real pain, and real fears, and who will treat you with care and respect. I want to share with you a few cautionary tales to give you a sense of what can happen if you don't take the time to put your lawyer on trial a little.

1. Sara had an attorney who never sent her a bill or a single court document. She was really distraught over her divorce and didn't have it in her at the time to go through the hassle of firing him and getting a new attorney, which she really needed to do. When she asked him questions he would make excuses, telling her it was all taken care of or that her husband's attorney was not getting back to him. He blamed her ex's attorney for everything. She lost thousands of dollars because he gave her the wrong information and let her agree to things that really screwed her.

It turns out he was a single dad who was having major ex-wife problems of his own. His personal situation was clouding his judgment around her case. She may not have been able to get this information up front, but where she went wrong was in not standing up for herself when she sensed he was not acting in her best interests. Even though you may need to hire someone to represent you in court, you are your own best advocate. Don't forget that! Fight for what you know you deserve, not just in the divorce settlement, but in how you are treated along the way.

2. Jane hired the kind of person we talked about at the beginning, only I'd call her a different type of animal: a shark. She pushed back against the other attorney, didn't take any crap, and demanded what she thought her client deserved. You might think that's okay as long as they are on your side and not representing your ex. You'd be wrong. Sure, she was fighting hard for Jane and knew that you never leave anything on the table

in a negotiation; but, her tactics were only stirring up conflict and unnecessary animosity between Jane and her ex. He changed his mind about everything they had agreed on before getting attorneys because he all of a sudden felt like she was trying to take him to the cleaners even though it wasn't her doing; it was her shark of an attorney smelling blood in the water.

Divorce is hard and painful enough as it is. If you have outside people getting you and your ex more upset and at each other's throats, what could be a relatively reasonable and respectful process suddenly becomes a long, drawn-out battle where no one actually wins. Don't let your emotions get in the way and give up your voice in the process. Let your attorney do what they are good at . . . within reason. If you think they are provoking your ex or his attorney to an unnecessary fight, stand up for yourself and insist on making decisions based on what is right and fair rather than what puts one in the WIN column.

3. Lola got her attorney from the bargain bin. She couldn't really afford much and had to limit how much time her attorney could spend on the case. She asked him to file standard divorce papers and keep it as straightforward as possible. The problem was her ex had plenty of money and his attorney took advantage of that and bombarded them with documents and dragged everything out. The attorney wasn't inept, but he also wasn't skilled enough to keep up with everything or combat their petty tricks. She ended up agreeing to far less than was fair just so she could get the divorce settled and end the piling up of billable hours she couldn't afford.

You may have no way around this kind of situation if you don't have much money for an attorney, and you may have to make a hard choice like Lola did just to have it all over. But, if you can, before you actually file for divorce, take the time to prepare financially for what is coming. (We'll talk in more detail about that a little later.)

WHAT YOU NEED

Make sure you ask the right questions of your attorney so you know your rights and responsibilities before you head into court. Understand what you can expect from the process.

It's really beneficial at the initial consultation to obtain as many answers to questions that you may have, because if you need any answers later, you will have to pay for those questions! One small question can cost the equivalent of a new pair of shoes. You need to make out a list of things that you're concerned about.

1. *Fee Structure*: Do they bill for each hour spent on your case or is it a fixed fee? Before you get into your particular case, please find out their hourly rate or fixed fee. Do not say one word about your case until you know the numbers. If their fees range from 300-500 per hour and you tell them you have money, you know you won't be paying 300. Remember this can take *years* to finalize, so you must be really clear about the financial implications this can have for you.

2. *Procedures*: What procedures do they require in your state to file for the divorce. You want to ask for a rough timeline, although they really don't have a clue and it depends on the complexity of your situation, or how big a dick your ex is going to be. If you know he isn't going to do this in an amicable way, when the lawyer tells you his guesstimate, add on six months.

3. *Custody*: I pray you don't have kids, but if you do this is the most important aspect of your divorce. Who cares if you lose the eight-dollar dish when you divide up the assets, you can lose your children part of the time. If he's a good dad who loves his kids, and wants

50/50, this is the best option. Child custody prolongs divorce proceedings, and you really should try avoid complicating it.

4. *Alimony*: How long have you been married, did you stay home to raise your children's, what's the discrepancy between your earnings? Each state has different rules.

5. *Assets*: It's important to ask the legal framework for splitting assets, it is usually a straightforward formula for allocating the assets; but, again, each state varies.

MONEY FOR NOTHING

And, chicks are not free . . . men will attest to that in a divorce. I met a guy who was divorced three times and he told me he left all his exes very comfortable. He was super well off and said, "I love women. What better things do I have to spend my money on?" Wow, a man who doesn't fight to hurt someone he used to love is rare. I was so intrigued. He didn't even have kids with the last two wives he gave millions to.

As you go through the legal process of divorce you are going to see the costs pile up before you even get to court, and you will look at the invoices your attorney sends and become convinced this is a lot of money for nothing. You won't be entirely wrong, but there are a lot of expenses associated with legal representation you should understand so you can be smart about what you ask your attorney to do for you.

Let me say first that I think there should be a cap in place on the amount of money you can spend on a divorce. The way our legal system is structured, it is possible to spend thousands and thousands of dollars on things you will never see. A cap would do a couple of things: 1) It would force lawyers to get the case settled ASAP; and 2) it would give both parties an equal footing and keep their games to a minimum. Why won't this ever happen? Because angry, cray-cray people get pleasure out of hurting their exes and want to see them suffer, and lawyers make way too much money off of people going through the pain of divorce. If the bad attorneys smell money and can milk a client for all they have, why would they do the right thing when the law is set up so they can make thousands and thousands of dollars off of it? Lemme tell ya, those lawyers ain't dumb. And no I'm not slamming on good lawyers, if you can make money in any profession, you take it. I'm just saying some sort of cap will protect the single mom where she can afford to get what she needs and not be too stressed out in the process so she can still take care of her kids.

So, what can you expect? Well, let me say off the bat that there are online documents and legal kits that help you file all the right papers, and for some circumstances that can work. BUT, that's only if your ex agrees to do this simply and not involve an attorney, and you don't have kids. If there is anything about your relationship or family situation that could possible complicate things, don't try a DIY divorce.

Most attorneys in LA charge a minimum $5,000 retainer. As they perform work for you they will deduct from that $250 to $450 for each hour of their time. But, here's the thing to remember: most attorneys break their time down into 15-minute increments, so if you send an email to your attorney to bitch about each and every thing your ex says to the kids that you don't like, your attorney will charge you for having to read and respond to that. So, make sure it's worth a minimum of $62.50 to complain to your lawyer about the fact that the ex said you were a nag. Your better option is to just keep a journal where you document everything you think your attorney should know—make sure to include dates, times, locations, and any other important details—and give it to them once a week or once a month so your retainer isn't getting nickel-and-dimed away before you find yourself in front of a judge.

In addition to the cost of hiring an attorney, there will be other fees and things that come up and have to come out of your pocket. There are filing fees that run around $200. If a sheriff or process server delivers the divorce petition to your ex, you are looking at another $35 to $100. Also, just because you have an attorney on retainer it doesn't mean they aren't going to find other ways to get money from you. In addition to their time, they will charge you for their paralegal's time, for couriers who run documents to the courthouse for them, for the copies of all of the paperwork they make for you and for the court and for your ex and his attorney.[4]

I can't tell you every expense you will encounter. Each state has its own unique requirements and, depending on where you live, the costs could be lower or much higher. So, it is on you to have a very specific conversation with your attorney about the typical costs and what they charge and how they bill for hours so you have some idea of what to expect and can budget accordingly.

The bottom line is this money stuff is going to feel like adding insult to injury, but it is an unavoidable part of the road you are on. The more informed you are, the better prepared you will be, and the more questions you ask ahead of time, the less sticker shock you'll experience later on.

THE WAY IT IS

It's just the way it is, some things will never change. The first thing you need to understand about filing for divorce is that everyone is going to test boundaries. Your attorney will push you to prepare you for the questions you'll get from the judge/mediator and from your ex's attorney. The other attorney is going to push for what they think is the best arrangement for their client (although, keep in mind that the rule of thumb in any negotiation is that you ask for more

4   http://info.legalzoom.com/average-cost-uncontested-divorce-20665.html

than what you want so that when you have to give ground you're not actually giving up anything you really want). Your ex is going to push your buttons because they are coming from a place of hurt and anger. The judge is going to expect everyone to act like grownups and find a reasonable solution, even though they know that's a big fantasy.

Keeping in mind what I just said about the rule of thumb for negotiations, there are two crucial points where you need to have an honest conversation with yourself about what you really want and what is a deal-breaker for you. The first time you need to ask yourself those question is when you decide to hire an attorney and move forward with your divorce. You are going to be in a certain frame of mind and will be pretty adamant about what you believe you deserve and where you intend to stand your ground. The second time you need to have that talk with yourself is after you meet with your attorney and get a strong dose of reality about your situation, what it's going to cost financially and emotionally to meet your list of demands. Maybe you can't realistically live on less than a certain amount of spousal or child support and that's your bottom line. Or you firmly believe your children need to stay in the same school and so visitation with your ex who has moved out of town has to be restricted to school breaks. These may sound like reasonable demands to you, but your ex might not agree. You may also find that your expectation isn't as reasonable as you see it and your attorney will help you understand that the judge is not going to award you $5,000 per month in support if your ex-husband only brings in $6,000. You may have to adjust your perspective on visitation if the kids have a good relationship with their father and he only lives in the next town over.

You are going to have to sit down with yourself to figure out where you can give a little and where you absolutely have to hold the line and insist that this is just the way it is. After that, you're going to have to accept that your ex is also going to have his "that's just the way it is" position as well. Hopefully you'll find there is room in the middle where you can meet and discover that some things can change. While the ugly side of divorce is that it boils down to a really cynical business negotiation where the parties have deeply personal insights to leverage a better deal, it is an opportunity to find your capacity for compassion and compromise that can lead you to better choices—even if that is only for the innocents caught up in the whole debacle. Sometimes it's better to just cut your losses and walk away.

CHLOE

Chloe had a lot of money and was very successful; her husband, on the other hand, was not. They were married for fifteen years when she found out her husband had a whole other family on the side. They didn't have children, but he did with another woman while they were married. When she found out about his second family, his son was already ten years old. He bought them a house with her money, paid his child support with her money, and used to go fly to see them with her money, or fly them in to see him. Anywho, during the divorce, her attorney was honest with her. He thought it would be best to just pay him off to leave. Her husband was going to suck her dry in legal fees and end up with a lot of money anyway. This marriage mistake cost her $300,000 and caused severe emotional issues. But, she did the smart thing and paid him off, even though that was so unfair! I get livid when I hear about people still having to pay alimony or give money to people who broke a marital contract. If you broke a business contract you would get sued, but in a marriage contract you still have to pay. WTF?

BAD BAD BILLY

Bad Bad Billy was off to war serving our country, but he

was also serving one of the female soldiers while he had a beautiful wife at home with two small children. During the divorce he made her life a living hell and refused to help financially. Yes, she could have taken him to court, but she knew he would stop at nothing to hurt her and make sure didn't get money. Even though she wasn't the one out having affairs and was home taking care of their children alone. She cut her loses and walked away. He had a lot of family money that she was entitled to, and they bought some properties during the marriage, but she knew it wasn't worth fighting a cray-cray man. Point being, sometimes you just need to cut your losses for your sanity.

THE REFLEX

Seriously, try not to use it or bruise it. Yeah, the reflex—the knee-jerk reaction—you are bound to have at many points during your divorce, 9 times out of 10, is going to be a bad call. There is no way around the fact that you are operating from a place of emotions that are all over the place and off the charts, so you are bound to over-react and be answered with a question mark. *What was I thinking? Why did he do that? How can I get back at him?*

There are a couple of ways to avoid making mistakes in these reflex moments. The first, and the really big one, is to work on yourself—on keeping yourself grounded and calm, keeping perspective, and breathing deeply . . . A LOT. Remembering that you have no control over what someone else does, only how you respond to it, is key. You've probably heard the distinction between reacting and responding—a reaction happens in an instant and without any thought, and a response is thoughtful and measured and done after taking a pause to be sure about the best way to deal with a situation. You are going to find yourself reacting more than you'd like as you go through your divorce, so be mindful of this tendency so you aren't burning down the village over his request to have St. Patrick's Day every other year added to the visitation even though your side of the family is more Irish than his.

The other tool you have at your disposal is your attorney. While you don't want to run to them with every complaint because they are even more expensive than most therapists and not nearly as equipped for dealing with this kind of shit, you can check with them before you freak out over the process server standing outside your kids' school waiting to catch you in the carpool line. They can talk you down off of some ledges just by preparing you ahead of time for certain tactics that may be used to throw you off your game, and they can give you the comfort of knowing that you have recourse if someone steps over the line and how they plan to address it. It's about to get crazy, so just remember to call on the people and influences around you that keep you centered; and, I can't say this enough, just . . . BREATHE.

LEAN ON ME

Because divorce is a highly emotionally-charged experience you are going to need someone to lean on since you will have many moments when you aren't strong. You will need a lot of guidance and emotional support to get through it. As I pointed out in the last section, your attorney is a great source of information to keep you from panicking unnecessarily and for keeping you focused on what you need to do. But, they can't be your confidante and your therapist too; nor should they be.

Call on those people who have been in your life all along to help you along the way. Don't shut people out and hide away in your depression. Ask for help. If you find that your family is too close to the situation to be objective or you don't know yet which friends you'll get in the divorce, you may need to seek outside help. There are professionals who can help you deal with the emotions that have and will continue to come up. There are also support groups full of people who have been down this same road and have a wealth of experience you can learn from, though sometimes it's more a matter of "Don't do what I did." You are not an island. Even if you would like to think you are Wonder Woman, you don't have to do this alone. Call on the people in your life who will be there to help you carry on and you'll get through it.

SHAKEDOWN

When you split up your marriage, it isn't just the relationship and the people in it that get divided. You also have to divvy up all of your stuff. And you won't believe the things that all of a sudden become important that you didn't care about before. You might even feel like you're getting a shakedown as you are nickel-and-dimed to death by your ex. It reminds me of the scene in *When Harry Met Sally* when Harry is having a meltdown after seeing his ex and all of the stuff that was backed up comes pouring out. He tells Jess and Marie, "Right now, everything is great . . . But, you gotta know that sooner or later you're going to be screaming at each other about who's gonna get this dish. This $8 dish is going to cost you $1,000 in phone calls to the legal firm of 'That's Mine, This Is Yours!'" Then he says, "Do me a favor, for your own good, put your name in your books right now . . . because, someday, believe it or not, you'll go fifteen rounds over who's going to get this . . . stupid wagon wheel, Roy Rogers, garage sale coffee table!"[5]

You may not think you'll be those people—the type who would fight over meaningless stuff. But, hell, you also probably never thought you'd be the couple getting a divorce, and yet, here you are. So, what is the deal with splitting up your possessions during a divorce?

---

5   Ephron, Nora. *When Harry Met Sally.* Film. Rob Reiner. Columbia Pictures, 1989.

CHAPTER 5

Nolo.com explains that divorcing couples often decide how they will divide their property instead of leaving it to the judge. But, if they can't agree, they'll have to put that decision in the judge's hands and they will use state law rules to divide the property, which typically falls into one of two categories: community property or equitable distribution. Debts are also included in the stuff you have to split in a divorce and the same guidelines apply, but I don't see too many people arguing for a bigger portion of that!

Community property is the stuff owned equally by both spouses and typically acquired during the marriage. Separate property is what you bring into the marriage. Community property is generally divided equally between the spouses, and may be determined based on the length of the marriage. Separate property is kept by the individual who owns it. The states that use the community property rule are: Alaska, Arizona, California, Idaho, Louisiana, Nevada, New Mexico, Texas, Washington, Wisconsin, and Puerto Rico.

All of the other states, use the equitable distribution rule where all of the assets and earnings accumulated during the marriage are divided equitably, but that doesn't necessarily mean they are split equally. Also, dividing property does not necessarily mean a physical division. You might just end up with a percentage of the value of something. A good example of this is your house, and that leads me to another point I want to make.[6]

If you can afford it financially, I don't think anyone should remain in the home they shared with their ex because it's not healthy emotionally. Although, if you're going to lose a lot of money, or have children who need to stay in their school system, keep the house, but I would recommend giving it a major facelift. You're going to need to find ways to heal in the environment you shared with the person you

6   https://www.nolo.com/legal-encyclopedia/dividing-proper-ty-debt-during-divorce-faq.html

loved and sometimes that starts with erasing all of the details
that remind you of what you shared together there.

If you are fighting for certain assets or possessions
because you feel like it's the way to get back at your ex for all
of the pain and suffering he caused, I have one thing to say:
let the universe take away their stuff and balance the scales.
You should always strive to end every relationship with love
and respect whether the other person is or not. You can only
control your behavior, but you do have control over it, and
being vindictive is no way to earn good karma for your next
relationship.

ANYTHING FOR YOU
Everyone likes to think that putting the children first is a
no-brainer. I mean who in their right mind wouldn't say,
"Anything for you, anything that will keep you safe and happy
and protected from this pain." Unfortunately, most adults get
so wrapped up in their own pain that they, at some point
along the way, end up making a choice or saying something
that is about as far from being in their children's best interests
as it gets. This doesn't make you a bad parent; it makes you
a hurting, lost, and fearful parent.

WHAT HAVE YOU DONE FOR ME LATELY
I know your ex probably hasn't done anything for you lately,
but I hope he's doing the 50/50 for his kids. Child custody is
probably the second worst issue that comes up with a divorce.
My belief is that, unless their safety and wellness is in danger,
all parents should have a 50/50 agreement. However, I also
feel that if it turns out that the child is spending most of
that time with a new significant other or a hired caregiver,
the parent not showing up should have their time restricted.
Parenting is supposed to be a partnership, and divorce doesn't
change that. Parents shouldn't be allowed to just leave their

children and not take half the responsibility, or feel that their job is more important than their ex . . . unless, it's an absolute emergency that is more important than raising children, and I'm clueless on what that would even be. If one parent chooses not to do the 50/50 because somehow they feel their job or the new wife is more important than their children, they should be giving a lot of help financially to their ex who is raising them. Even if you aren't a team as spouses, you should be a team as parents, working together to raise a child, equally.

DEVIL INSIDE

Child support also creates a lot of resentment and the devil inside of some men comes out and tells them it's okay to hurt their children by not paying it. It makes you wonder, wonder, wonder how some people sleep at night. I'm amazed at how many men I hear of who say they don't mind providing for their kids, but just don't want to have to give the money to the mother of their kids who's taking care of them. In case there are any men reading my book, let me just give a little tough love right now. GROW THE FUCK UP!! If your ex really is not using the money for the kids' care, you have legal recourse, but just because you resent the fact that she is still getting money from you in any form is no excuse to punish your kids. You know very well what it costs to run a household if you paid a single bill in your married life, so think about what your ex is going through to keep the household going with a drastic reduction in income. And don't begrudge her the occasional mani/pedi. She's working hard to take care of your kids. You should be giving her spa gift certificates every month if she's taking care of your kids alone! She deserves and needs pampering occasionally. (Of course I am not talking about the woman who only takes care of her own needs and sends your kids to school without lunch money and is always out having fun instead of really parenting; but, if my experience is any indicator, the ratio of men who shirk their support responsibilities compared to the number of that type of mother is about 10,000:1.) Women, I can't let you off the hook entirely though because there are some of you out there who do expect your ex to foot the bill so you don't have to work and still have a nanny. You have your own responsibilities in this and have to show up and make some sacrifices too, even if he did fuck the nanny, his play toys at work, or your best friend. I know it hurts and sucks when your life gets turned upside down, but this stuff happens to people every day and we all have to find a way to get through it and start over.

The irony, of a man screwing over the mother of his children with alimony and child support is that she is going to get a lot of his money when he dies anyway. Here me out! If a man screws the mother of his children over financially and she struggles to make ends meet and take care of their kids, the kids will have the responsibility of taking care of her when she gets older. If he goes first, (which is likely because women tend to outlive men and God might not let him live that long) the money he leaves to them will be in the pool of the resources they use to cover her long-term care expenses. Men have a hard time understanding that their money will always be connected to the wife they have children with. Those kids will benefit from her having money, and living a good life, which he should want. I know, a cray-cray man doesn't like hearing that, but they can't have their cake and eat it too. It's not how life works.

TARZAN BOY

Tarzan boy cheated on his wife so many times that I couldn't even keep up with the list of women he told me about. His wife kicked him out and he married some woman from work and took a job far away. He had five homes and plenty of money, yet would fight the mother of his children over every penny of child support and wasn't helping with the parenting. I asked him if he cared about his kids and he said yes, but he wasn't willing to take care of them while they were living with his ex. His kids lived in a small apartment and their mom worked three jobs. He said if his ex doesn't want to support the kids and take care of them, he and his new wife would be glad to take them. His new wife would be glad to stay home and raise his kids. So, he was willing to take his kids away from their mom who had been a stay-at-home mom and raised them while he was working and out having affairs. I didn't even know what to say to that. When he did see his kids, he spoiled the shit out of them so they would think he was a good guy while he was fucking their mother over left and right. I see this one all the time!

Not all men are like this, I know. I've known some men who make sure that their ex and the kids are set up in a nice home, in a good school district, and receive significantly more in child support than what the court decides they should. Some guys do the right thing because they messed up during the marriage, and others just want the best for their kids and their mother who is taking care of them.

So, the message here is don't make these fundamental responsibilities a source of conflict and the thing that keeps you from settling your divorce as peacefully as possible.

Divorce is never easy. Ending a relationship you chose for better or worse is going to be painful—you'll feel like a failure; you'll feel betrayed; you'll feel like you are letting your kids down, your whole family down—so why use the legal system that will suck your bank accounts dry to cause even more pain?

Chapter 6
NOVEMBER RAIN

Sometimes you need time all alone. Sometimes you may even need some time on your own. It's hard starting over and facing the realization that nothing lasts forever. If you are on the other side of your divorce, take a deep breath now that the major drama is over. The worst is behind you. If you are still in the middle of your divorce, make time to do this self-care to help you get through with less stress. Take things slow and understand that you shouldn't expect yourself to be over everything right now and you're going to need a lot of time to heal.

Give yourself a chance to fully recover. Take it one day at a time and be as loving to yourself as possible. You are the love of your life. It really doesn't matter who loves you as long as you love you. You have to live with yourself for the rest of your days on this tiny planet, and it should be lived loving yourself. You're not perfect and neither is anyone else. But, you have two choices: you can focus on fixing the things you hate about yourself or you can accept them. If you made mistakes in the past, stop beating yourself up. If you were the one who cheated on your husband, or messed up the marriage, apologize to him and forgive yourself. We all mess up and do stupid things. Make a commitment to change and make that change even if it wasn't your fault. But, for now, let's dig into working on healing from your divorce transition. Do as many of the things I suggest that resonate with you, and definitely try the things that make you a little uncomfortable so you can have some new experiences and challenge your beliefs.

LISTEN TO YOUR HEART

Laying low and giving yourself time to heal is one of the most important things you can do right now. I know the tendency is to listen to all of the unsolicited advice people are hurling at you—maybe you're reading some advice books too—and a lot of it may be conflicting. Your head is a big jumble of should's and shouldn'ts and you don't know where to turn. I'm going to tell you right now to listen to your heart because there's nothing else you can do that will be any better for you and your situation. You instinctively know what is going to work for you, but you are going to have to work on trusting your instincts. I know that may be easier said than done when you are questioning everything, especially your judgment in matters of the heart; but, you are the best person to decide what you need to heal.

I will warn you that there are some decisions that feel like they are coming from your heart but don't feel right deep down. These are usually ideas motivated by your ego or your wounded pride. If this happens, stop a minute, ask yourself if what your heart is telling you to do is really going to help you in the long run or end up causing more pain. Then, wait thirty minutes, an hour, whatever amount of time seems right, and see if you still want to do that thing. If you haven't been drinking or going on four days of no sleep because you've been crying, and it still seems like a good idea, go ahead.

BROKEN WINGS

If your divorce was difficult for you, you may feel like you have broken wings and may never learn to fly again, not just in relationships, but in most areas of your life. Here are some tips to help you get really centered to be the best possible you and maybe get into a new relationship in time.

1. *Silent Morning* - The greatest thing about meditation

is you can't do it wrong and it's free. You don't have to buy anything or hire anyone. It requires only a small amount of your time and can be practiced anywhere. Guided meditation courses are a good start. You can go on YouTube and even get free videos.

After your divorce sometimes your mind is confused and racing. It really does help to shut the hell up for a few minutes. Sometime you can really get a clear picture of all the stupid things you are thinking about for absolutely no reason.

There are so many benefits such as developing compassion, love, patience, generosity and forgiveness. Meditation is used to clear the mind, which will help alleviate depression, and anxiety, which are common feeling during a divorce.

Meditating fifteen minutes a day has taught me to be more self-aware during the day, and how stupid my thinking is a lot of the time. One day, I really wanted to meditate but my thoughts were all over the place. I couldn't stop thinking of this clown I saw eating yogurt on a beach. I had to stop meditating and go have a glass of wine. But, that's the beauty of meditation, if you fail one day, you can do other things that work for stress relief.

I do try to be a good meditator because I know it really works even if you get a few glimpses of peace. There are many ways to meditate, just do whatever is easiest for you, remember you're just trying to become more aware of yourself and your surroundings, not become the Buddha.

2. *Lay Your Hands on Me* - My belief is that most of our diseases are stress related, and doing things to alleviate stress, such as massage, will make a huge difference in your health.

What is massage? Only the greatest stress reliever ever! Massage may seem like a luxury, but it has numerous therapeutic effects and should be thought of as part of your routine health care regimen. It's been proven to lessen depression and anxiety. Divorce usually has some depression and anxiety that goes along with it.

During your divorce you need to utilize everything possible that makes you feel better. If you can decrease anxiety, enhance the quality of your sleep, improve your energy and concentration, increase your circulation and reduce fatigue, why not get regular massages?

The cost of massages has gone down. In LA, you can go down any street and get a Thai massage for $50. I found a place I love; granted, they have a sign when you walk in that says they don't perform sex acts during the massage. Nonetheless it was a better massage than some of the really beautiful massages for $150 in Beverly Hills, plus the no sex sign makes me happy. I read the sign out loud to the Thai lady and laugh as I pay. She looks at me like I'm cray-cray. Life is about being happy and I do everything possible to keep me happy.

3. *Here Comes the Rain Again* - Be around water even if it's just a fountain. I'm blessed to live in California near the beach, although Lake Shrine is one of my favorite places to go when I need to think and reflect what is going on my life. It has beautiful gardens and a natural spring-fed lake. The swans, ducks, koi, turtles, butterflies, trees, and flowers from all around the world will help you relax. It's like you're in another world, a peaceful world where problems don't exist. This sanctuary holds a portion of Mahatma Gandhi's ashes enshrined.

If you don't live near Lake Shrine find a place near you. Our world is so beautiful, so it shouldn't be hard to find a beautiful place near you and make it your spot.

You can take your problems there and figure them out or chose not to bring your problems with you and just enjoy your sanctuary. Neither choice is right or wrong, good or bad. It's all about what is going to bring you back to happiness and love, and only you know the answer. Hanging near Gandhi's ashes does it for me.

I get a little freaked out by TMN (too much nature) but others seem to enjoy it. I do believe that this is probably the most powerful way to cleanse the aura. Being in nature is very grounding, whether you are gardening, walking, or sitting by a lake or ocean. While going through a divorce, being outside is essential, especially if you are a bit depressed.

4. *Body Language* - When I was going through my divorce I saw a therapist who was a divorced single mom. I went twice a week for a year. I highly recommend that you find a therapist who has been divorced and has kids if you have kids. I'm sure therapists are okay who have the textbook knowledge of divorce and kids, but I'm the type of girl who wants people who have had the experience as opposed to having just read about it.

I like female gynecologists because when I tell them about my lady center, they 100 percent understand me. They know what cramps feel like, and if they have kids, they know what having a baby feels like. They have the textbook knowledge and a lady center. Get me? I don't want someone with a penis telling me about my lady center. Always hire people who understand YOU! It simply makes sense.

Post-divorce counseling is imperative if you want to enter into a healthy new relationship at some point. History tends to repeat itself unless you change. If you grow, change and take responsibility for your part in the bad marriage even if it was just your fault for staying in it.

The next relationship will benefit from your growth.

Please don't let needing therapy make you feel weak. It's actually a strength admitting that you do. Everyone needs therapy after a divorce! You experience loss, whether it was good loss or bad loss. We all tend to learn more from our mistakes than our successes. Get a divorced therapist who will help you go over your mistakes and learn everything you needed to learn from them. If you can't afford counseling, many cities have community health centers that offer counseling services for a very low fee. You can even check local churches.

If you're really sad and don't know anyone going through a divorce it may be a good idea to join a divorce support group. It's a good way to know that you're not alone and be around people who understand your pain. You can cry and tell your story and hear other stories to help you heal. You may find some really good friends in one of these groups.

If you're not really upset over your divorce and you have good friends to talk to and family that supports you, you may not want to go. These groups are healing but can be depressing. Hearing depressing stories is not going to lift you out of your sadness or depression. Hearing love stories will keep you positive and at a higher attraction level for good things to come your way. You have to figure out where you are at in your healing and what is good for you.

These groups should let everyone tell their horror story to get it out and heal, but they should also have to find one love story during the week and share that as well. If you're not sure, go ahead and try out the divorce support groups, and if they feel good stay; if not, get out quickly. Al-Anon is also a great program that has helped millions of people. If you don't feel like going, you can read some of their literature online; it's very healing.

They recommend amazing books.

5. *The Ghost In You* - I love going to see my psychic. Psychics get a bad rap because there are so many dishonest ones. Just a heads up, there also are dishonest dentists who tell you need crowns instead of fillings, dishonest car salesmen who tell you need new tires, breaks, nuts, bolts, and screws. There are dishonest financial advisors who take your money. The list can go on; it's in every profession! Don't be hating the psychics!

You need a reputable psychic who can help you build your intuition—we are all naturally psychic, we just don't know how to use it. I don't believe any psychic can tell the future 100 percent because things change, but they can help you understand why things happen and what's going on right now. It's really helpful when you feel like your intuition may be a bit off due to a stressful divorce. When you're not thinking clearly it's hard to get through the day, let alone understand your intuition and make good choices.

I've received a lot of good info about business associates who were helping me and hurting me and amazing insight on some of the men I dated. All of the information I received about my ex was very accurate! My favorite psychic is Christina Cooper! She is a sweet older lady who reads you through cards. I usually see her once a year and I ask her about my new job and my new boyfriend. She thinks I will meet someone and get married when I'm able to let love in, so I'm thinking, after what I went through, when I'm around seventy. She's been telling me about a guy named John with blue/green eyes for years. Let's see what happens.

Even if you're not a believer in psychics, I'm asking you to step outside of your box and give it a try. Just don't go to anyone that is not completely reputable. Never go to someone on the street or that has a sign in a window. The best psychics usually have a great reputation, have been on TV, or have written a popular book. Unfortunately, it can be hard to get an appointment with them and they are super expensive.

6. *New Moon On Monday* - Everyone should have his or her own personal astrological chart done. I'm an Aquarius, but I have more Scorpio in me. I never felt like an Aquarius, and having my chart done explained my personality to a tee. My chart helped me understand myself better. Astrology is one of the most comprehensive ways to uncover who you are. You should be uncovering away during this transition. It's time to get to know you again.

A thorough analysis of your chart will help you understand your gifts and your shortcomings. We all have great qualities and not so great qualities, which can help transcend your weaknesses and maximize your strengths. Astrology is another tool that will help you look deep within yourself. Knowing and loving yourself inside and out will certainly make your life easier and all of your relationships stronger.

7. *When I Hear Music* - Sound therapy won't make you dance, but it will make you heal. Sound healing is a proven way to increase your health by reducing stress and a deeper connection to everything around us. It's been documented that it assists in the healing process for chemotherapy patients. Going through a divorce is very stressful; the bowls frequency helps reduce depression. Most of the day the frequency of our brain waves is in beta. Tibetan Healing Bowls move us over to alpha and theta frequencies, which are the frequencies that create peaceful states. If you want to increase your intuition and psychic abilities the frequency can't be in a beta state.

The medical field can now measure and confirm sound therapy as a means to healing. Sound is an energy that creates the vibration in which people can heal from disease. Go on YouTube and look up some sound therapy. Listen to it at night as you fall asleep. It really works. Give it a month and see what happens. If you don't think it did anything after a month don't do it, but I bet you will find it does help, most people do. If you're super angry and negative right now, nothing is going to work for you until you lighten up a bit, so use the slogan "fake it until you make it" and listen to some damn sound waves.

8. *Pressure* – Jin Shin Jyutsu is a style of acupressure that works with a set of twenty-six points along energy pathways. It's an ancient healing practice that a Japanese healer rediscovered in the 20th Century. It was found that Jin Shin Jyutsu was widely known in antiquity-before the time of Buddha, Moses, and the Kojiki.

When a pathway becomes blocked energy stagnates and has the potential to create imbalance along the entire pathway. When the balance is restored along the pathways you will experience physical, mental, and spiritual harmony.

I wasn't sure what to think of this when I tried it, but it seriously worked. If I could've afforded more sessions at the time, I would've gone every week. I had five sessions and it was amazing.

9. *One More Shot* - The only needle going into me is to take blood when I'm sick and for Botox because I look ten years younger. Acupuncture involves inserting thin needles at strategic points on your body. Chinese medicine explains it as a technique for balancing the flow of energy known as qi or Chi. Inserting these needles at specific points helps to restore the energy flow and your body will re-balance. I've had numerous friends say

they love acupuncture and experience healing from it. If you're not afraid of the needle, go for it! Just please don't post it on Facebook, Instagram, tweet it, or put it on any other social media. Keep your injections private.

10. *Pure Energy* - Yes, spiritual cleansing is important. You must clear your aura and get rid of any negative energy Clearing your aura is normal (in LA). When our species is more advance in the future I bet it will be as normal as brushing your teeth. I know a lot of people think this is a bunch of BS; but, why don't you try it and see for yourself? There are different ways to clear your aura—crystals, sage, sea salt baths, essential oils and being in nature.

- I'm a big fan of crystal work. I'm a fan of black or green tourmaline. If you wear it as a pendant or keep it somewhere on your body it protects your aura by shielding it from unwanted energy. Other crystals that can protect the aura are fire agate, smokey quartz, labradorite, and black kyanite.
- You need to sage the hell out of your house, especially if it's the house where you and your ex lived together. Negativity energy is everywhere, like dust in your house; it coats everything and continues to build up. I walk around my house with the sage and really let the smoke rise up to the ceiling and make sure I get each corners in my house really well. I don't recommend staying in the house you once shared with someone, but if you have to stay for your kids or financial reasons, break out the sage.
- Essential oils are great for purifying, grounding, and uplifting the energy of your aura. You can apply it directly to your skin or add it to a diffuser, which will also cleanse your home. My favorite is

cedarwood, but bergamot and orange are great
aura cleansers.

- Sea salt baths are really therapeutic. If you
  have a fabulous bathtub, soak away my friend!
  I heard it's preferred to go into the ocean, but I
  personally don't go into water if I can't see the
  bottom. I want to see what's going to bite me and
  kill me. Epsom salt or Dead Sea salt baths can
  be tremendously relieving and cleansing after a
  stressful day. It will clean, refresh, and revitalize
  the energy of the body.
- Get out in nature. Hiking, walking, or even sitting
  in nature will expose you to unseen elements that
  will have a positive effect on your brain. The ions
  emitted from electronics can wreak havoc on your
  body. Twenty minutes outside around nature can
  bring you and your fabulous body to a nice calm
  place.

Listen, you should be challenging yourself and getting
out of your comfort zone during this transition. It's time
to do different things, and if you really don't want to do
it, then you definitely should to see why your thoughts
are against it. Remember, your thoughts are just your
thoughts, it doesn't mean they are right. As you grow
your thoughts about things change. Whichever one of
these you want to do the least . . . start there! I went
camping, and if I can start there being scared of TMN
(too much nature) you can hold a crystal or rub some
damn oil on ya.

11. *Space in the Place* - Someone asked me what Feng Shui
really means and I guess the most simplistic answer is
it means to throw shit out. If you have too much stuff,
clutter, or, God forbid, things that remind you of your
ex, it blocks energy. This is an emergency in your home

just like a fire. You don't need to call the fire department unless you live in Santa Monica, California, where the firemen look better than Chippendale dancers. But, you don't have room for one of those handsome fellas until your space is cleared.

Everything in your home holds energy; to bring in positive energy it must have space. If everything is cluttered, old, and does not reflect who you are today, it needs to go, and go as soon as possible. This takes a lot of time and work but is so worth it. It's actually very liberating. If you can afford to hire a Feng Shui consultant, do it! If not, you can read plenty online and keep in mind the whole basis of this is to make room for energy to flow and feel happy in your space.

The billion-dollar interior decorating industry attests to the fact that beauty and comfort in our living environments is essential. Our surroundings affect our success, mental health, and relationships. The way objects are placed in your home affects your personal energy flow, which affects how you think, act, performs and succeed in your life

In English, *Feng Shui* means wind and water, the two most basic elements for human survival. All living things are composed of these two elements. It's an ancient Chinese art and science based on laws that govern the flow of energy. The energy is called Chi, or life force. Changing the Chi in your home creates positive changes in your life. That means, Feng Shui is the art of making your home into a harmonious flow of energy.

If Feng Shui doesn't resonate with you, just keep your house spotless and throw a ton of stuff out. You really don't need all the stuff you have. My psychic told me that I needed to clear out my house to make room for the things I want in life. I cleared a ton of old toys out of my kids' room and a bunch of divorce papers I never read, and my house felt lighter and happier inside. It worked like butter!

12. *You Can Do Magic* - Get a new scent! Smell is one of the most important things that you can change, and many of us over look this simple but necessary change! Smell evokes memory in a way no other sense can, and yet it is our most underused sense. Memory and smell are closely linked. In order to identify a smell, we have to remember it first and then place the object that it comes from into our vision. Studies have shown that recall can be enhanced if learning was done in the presence of odor. I smell everything! I'm like Toucan Sam the Fruit Loop guy. I follow my nose when I meet new people or go into new places. If something or someone smells bad, LEAVE!

The science dedicated to smell is called aromatherapy, which uses plants and herbs to help physical and mental pain. Essential oils contain healing properties and are natural, as opposed to perfume oils, which are artificially created. Essential oils will always remain the best bet for every lover of quality beauty products.

I love lavender; it's very therapeutic. It soothes and relaxes the body and mind, which is why it is often used at the spa. I always have lavender around me. Learn about aromatherapy; it's an interesting science. The simple fact that you can trick your mind into solving almost any physical and mental problem that you have through scent is amazing. I wore lavender for a while instead of perfume during my divorce. It works.

Try some essential oils and see which oil resonates with you. To make sure you get the optimum divorce stress relief try a few and see which one resonates with your mind and body.

Here are a few of the best essential oils for stress

relief:

- Lavender is one of the best essential oils for relaxation and health! It helps relieve stress, helps improve sleep, soothes muscle cramps, and rests the mind.
- Ylang Ylang is said to have great heart health benefits. It settles heart palpitations and balance hormones.
- Geranium is good for boosting your immune system, addressing menopause in women, soothing mature skin, calming nerves, uplifting and balancing the body.
- Frankincense is known to be one of the best options for putting your body and soul at ease.
- Bergamot is known to aid energy flow through your body. It is also known to for helping emotion-based issues such as anxiety, stress, and depression.
- Rose is good for calming nerves and PMS.

SMOKE ON THE WATER

A fire in the sky that clears energy is mandatory right now! Remember, incense is not just for hippies who smoke weed. The burning of incense has been used as part of religious ceremonies for millennia. Morphine, marijuana, and LSD have even been used in religious ceremonies. Burning of incense is a spiritual practice that has persisted across cultures and religions and now is shown to have healing properties for the brain.

New studies are coming out about burning frankincense, showing that it can help alleviate anxiety and depression. Frankincense may sound familiar to you. The wise men gave it to baby Jesus according to the book of Matthew. They gave him gold, myrrh, and frankincense. It was obviously seen as precious back in the day and now perhaps we are finding out why. Since Frankincense was considered as precious as gold and was good enough for baby Jesus, what the hell, why not try it out?

My favorite incense will always be Satya Sai Baba "Nag Champa." It's a blend of natural resins, herbs, flowers, and aromatic oils. The word Nag means, "snake" and "Champa" means flower. The name Snake Flower hints at the blossoming of awareness and the transformation power of the snake.

Burning incense is very symbolic because the slow rise of the smoke is supposed to go up to the kingdom of Heaven with our prayers. My house always smells like Nag Champa and everyone tells me how great the energy is in my home. If you really hate all the religious symbolism behind burning incense, buy it because it seriously is the only thing that takes out that nasty lingering smell of bacon.

RED RED WINE
You don't want that red, red wine staying too close to you because it can cause a lot of problems.

1. Alcohol can make you hungry by suppressing leptin, a hunger-regulating hormone. One margarita and nachos just ruined going to the gym all week. If that's not depressing enough, remember that alcohol itself is a depressant, so you're likely only going to end up amplifying the pain of your divorce.
2. Alcohol decreases B12, which can lead to fatigue. You may feel tired, but you aren't actually going to get good sleep because it affects your REM sleep—the sleep you need to feel rested and ready to conquer the world.
3. The effects of alcohol are stronger in women than men. The blood alcohol level of a woman who just drank the same quantity as a man will be higher because women have less water in their bodies, are smaller, and metabolize alcohol more slowly than men. Ladies you can't keep up with the men and shouldn't even try.

4. Alcohol decreases Vitamin A levels, which speeds up the aging process by causing a loss of collagen and elasticity, and increasing redness, dehydration, and puffiness. Plus, there are no nutrients and a lot of calories in alcohol. If you are spending money on collagen injections and drink alcohol, shame on you! You're wasting your money, which might be in short supply after your divorce!

When you are going through this transitional time, please limit your alcohol. Drinking really changes people's behaviors. I have so many friends who are quite good people, but if you give them one or two cocktails, they're out doing things they would never consider while sober. Women tend to turn to the bottle while going through a divorce to numb the pain.

I like the Buddhist point of view on alcohol: if you are on a quest to develop your mind and make positive changes in your life, you should refrain from consuming alcohol. Drinking while going through transition to avoid your problems distorts the mind, leaving little room to react wisely to emotions and sensations. Life is trying to teach us all the time, especially while we are going through a divorce. If our minds are not clear, how are we going to learn and how is all of this pain going to be worth it in the long run?

Remember, it's all about balance and taking good care of yourself while you are going through a tough time in your life. Have one drink to chill you out, a lot of water, and only a few nachos; moderation is the way to go! But, the day you see your ex's new girlfriend that he cheated on you with holding your small child... sure, go ahead drink the whole fucking bottle, and call me for support.

IT'S A MISTAKE

Okay, so I gave you some tips on taking care of yourself, but you still have some other issues you're working out. Maybe you are taking care of yourself but are lonely or still keep thinking of your ex. You have to really remind yourself he is your ex for a reason. Here are two major mistakes that women make after a divorce while they are trying to heal themselves. If you do these things, no judgment here, but it will delay your healing process and, God forbid, you get pregnant that's a whole new nightmare.

I NEED YOU TONIGHT

So, slide over here for a moment and hear me out ... sleeping with your ex never leads to anything good! I don't care if there is something about him that makes you sweat or scream with intense sexual pleasure. He may have had a lot of flaws, and you guys may have been all wrong for each other, except for this one area. And going from having regular access to the one that makes you sweat to being lonely and not sleeping is hard! You may kid yourself into thinking you need him tonight ... just for tonight ... and you can go back to normal once you scratch that itch. But, you know as well as I do that it's a slippery slope back into the same old relationship patterns that caused you to split up. Just don't even go there. You can resist the urge. There are toys if you need them, and there are plenty of other ways to distract yourself until the need passes. Start working out, pick up a hobby, do anything else that allows you to channel your sexual energy and frustration into something more useful than going down that rabbit hole.

And here's the thing, your ex is not Jesus. (If he was, you should never have left him because Jesus can turn water into wine; and who the hell leaves someone who could do that?) When the loneliness sets in and you are having moments of weakness you may tend to think your ex was a god! Everyone does it. When you were in the relationship with them they were driving you insane with all the horrible things that they were doing, but now that you are no longer together, what you remember is all the good times.

GOODBYE TO YOU

When people die everyone says really nice things about them in their eulogy. I'm sure the person who died was a real asshole to a few people in their lives. We just tend to have rose-colored rearview mirrors.

Go ahead and write out a list of all the bad things your ex did to you and how shitty it made you feel and keep it somewhere close so you can look at it the next time you're feeling tempted to reach out. A person who loves you and cares about you would never hurt you or leave you. They will always put you first and treat you with respect.

YOU'RE MY OBSESSION

Is he like a wild butterfly that you want to capture? Not so fast, I think some may be on the endangered species list and you don't want to go to jail for your obsession. Yup, it's completely normal to become obsessive, thinking about your ex constantly, and it doesn't have to be just sexual as we just discussed. It's what our brains do without our even thinking about it. Have you ever caught yourself going over and over something in your mind? It's probably long over and done, but your mind can't let it go. You can't change the outcome any, but you still obsess ... and that's just over what you ordered for lunch!

When your brain is in spin mode, you are going to replay everything about your marriage—what you could have done better, what he could have done better, how it ended, whether it should have ended—but you need to accept that it is what it is and not try to second-guess every detail.

It's okay to sit with those thoughts for a bit. Sorting it out will help you in all of your relationships going forward, but obsessing about it is different. That's over-analyzing every little detail, every single word exchanged, and it won't get you anywhere useful. Making peace with what happened as being in the past and looking for what you can learn from it is the only way to heal, grow, and move on from the obsessive thinking. I have gone over and over what I should've said, could've said, should not have said, and so on, but it's all a waste of my time when the present has so many more useful things I could be doing, such as working or hanging out with my kids or friends.

Let yourself go through the process without beating yourself up for it. Try to find the humor in how crazy your mind can be. Remember, you're going to look back at this time in your life someday and you won't remember how bad it hurt and think it was such a waste of time. You'll just see the healing that came from it.

GIRLS JUST WANT TO HAVE FUN
Let's end this chapter with some fun phone ideas. If you are the fun friend we all know and love you've probably done this already or think this is a brilliant idea. If you are not the fun friend, you really have to do this and make yourself laugh and shock your friends by showing them you are capable of stepping out of your box and doing something you would never do that you probably think is childish and stupid.

YOU CAN CALL ME AL
If you are mad at you ex you probably want to call him way more than Al right now. If you do, I'm not here to judge you! I recommend everyone change their ex's name in their cell phone to something spiritually meaningful to them to remind them to be peaceful during the conversation and to remember what they learned from the conversation, and have a nice laugh when Jesus calls you.

Remember, those who cause us the most pain are said to be our greatest spiritual teachers. Here are some good phone names; Jesus Christ, Krishna, Buddha, Osho, Dali Lama, Maya Angelo. Or if you're not feeling the spiritual thing, go with teachers from movies or TV such as Dewey Finn, Ms. Frizzle, Mr. Hand, Mr. Garrison, Ms. Norbury, Albus Dumbledore, or, my favorite, Mr. Miyagi! I actually find it quite amusing when my phone rings.

Now, the most important part: pick a good 80s ring tone as well! Here are a few of the most popular ones. If your ex cheated, the best ring tone is Orange Juice Jones, "The Rain." If you're an 80s girl like me you already know the lyrics; if not, go on YouTube and watch the video. Laughter will always be the best way to heal and get through a transition.

- "Tainted Love" by Soft Cell
- "Goodbye to You" by Scandal
- "The Breakup Song (They Don't Write 'Em)" by Greg Kihn Band
- "Beat It" by Michael Jackson
- "You Dropped a Bomb On Me" by Gap Band
- "The Rain" by Oran "Juice" Jones

Phase 3

THE FUTURE'S SO BRIGHT, I GOTTA WEAR SHADES

Now that the divorce is over, or soon to be over, I bet things have been going great and they're only getting better. I'm really excited for you and your bright future. No, this transition wasn't the easiest, and you may still be going through some shit right now, but you create your future by the choices you make and the people you let into your life. Choose well. Everything that is happening was meant to be so you can grow and learn. I hated when people told me that when I was getting divorced, but it's true.

Don't forget, you're never alone; you have an abundance of resources and spiritual guidance to handle the new crap that is going to come your way. You weren't happy married, or somebody else wasn't, so let's get cracking on being beyond happy as a single person. It's the only choice you have right now, so make the most of it.

How do you do that? By really getting to know yourself and what is best for you, finding a new love (when you're ready) with high values who treats you like butter, and helping others who don't know how difficult marriage can be to navigate those murky waters. This phase really is about your future being so bright, you gotta wear shades! So let's start figuring out what you really want, making that happen, and then sharing what you've learned along the way.

Chapter 7
ALMOST PARADISE

I bet when you planned your wedding right down to the little party favors you were going to put on the reception tables, you envisioned your life would be like paradise. Maybe you even went with a tropical island theme. (I won't hold it against you if you did. If it was the 80s it was almost expected.) But now your match made in Heaven went all to Hell. Perfect love really is hard to find; but, if you don't first find it for yourself, you won't be able to get the most out of any other love relationship you may experience. Our society places so much importance on being partnered with someone, and sometimes being single is seen as a sign that there is something wrong with you. Yes, it's challenging being single, but look at all the challenges that came with the marriage you just ended. You probably felt the pressure to get married so much that now you have this sense of failure in being single or divorced, which is really ridiculous. If you are happy being single, consider yourself lucky that you aren't having to put up with all the headaches that come with being in a relationship with someone, especially someone who carries baggage from their past.

If you're reading my book you probably already did the marriage thing, and, unfortunately, you have to be realistic about the probability that you may never meet another man you'd want to marry. Of course you will meet men because they are everywhere, and if you are attractive and have your shit together, you will get asked out a lot. But, you may not meet someone who will deserve to share in the precious time you have on this plant. Like Prince said, forever is a mighty long time.

Discovering things you love to do, finding good people

to spend your time with who don't want or need something from you, and taking your time to learn new things is the best option you have right now, and it really is almost paradise! So don't ask for more right now, you're knocking right at Heaven's door.

ONCE IN A LIFETIME

Most women usually do get married again, whether they should or not. It's can be really challenging being alone, and your singleness will probably be temporary, so enjoy the hell out of it. You have this once-in-a-lifetime opportunity right in front of you to get to know yourself in a new way, confront and fix your limitations, and really love yourself again. Seriously, if you don't feel comfortable being alone and spending time with yourself, others probably won't either. You may find you don't like a lot of things about yourself; but, when you learn to be patient, kind, and caring with yourself, you can change those things. This kind of personal growth can take a few years, but it's totally worth it. Becoming the best person you can possibly be is what life is all about. Whether you stay single or end up in another relationship, the best thing you can do for yourself at this stage is to give yourself time to heal and grow. If you decide flying solo is best for you, becoming your best means you will have a fantastic companion in yourself. And, if you want a new relationship, being your best and having confidence just improves your chances of success. This time is like getting to hit the reset button and have a fresh start (which doesn't happen often) if you make the most of it.

INTO THE GROOVE

It can take several years to get into the groove of being single again and get your shit together, especially if you were married for a long time. And, it's not just the boy who's going to have to prove his love to you when you start dating again; you have to prove your love for yourself first. The only way to do that is to give yourself permission for time out to work on yourself and discover areas where you need to improve. Don't be afraid to ask friends or family what they perceive your faults to be, but only do this when you are ready to accept honest answers and are willing to do the work necessary to fix whatever they bring to your attention.

I asked my friends to be brutally honest with me about things they might have observed about my personality or my behaviors. My friends know I really want to be the best person I can be and weren't afraid to tell me what they really thought because they knew I would never hold it against them and be thankful for their input. Count yourself lucky if you have friends who will tell you the truth to help you grow and not just what they think you want to hear. A friend who just tells you you're beautiful and great all the time is lying, because not one of us is that perfect. She's just afraid to tell you what she thinks. This kind of revelation is what you need to help you get into your groove and become the best you possible. This process will take as long as you need it to. Don't rush it to fit some arbitrary time table, and definitely not to meet anyone else's expectations. This time is about you.

STILL OF THE NIGHT

When you are sitting in the still of the night, does your mind wander to the last time you had sex? The last time you had good sex? To your regrets, sadness, anger, resentment, and all the other negative emotions you have been cycling through since your marriage started going south? If you let yourself get on that mental torture merry-go-round, it can be really easy to get trapped there. If you feel those emotions bubbling to the surface, stop yourself and ask, *What am I grateful for? What is good in my life that is bringing me joy, or at least bringing me through?* Possibly the fastest routes to healing and getting back your groove are through gratitude and positivity. Focus on those things and list them, with specifics, until the knot in your stomach and the tightness in your chest lessen and you can begin to enjoy the peace that lies in the stillness of the night instead of the loneliness and anxiety you've been experiencing.

After my divorce, as I fell asleep, my heart beat heavy and told me it needed more; but now, in the still of my night, I go to sleep thinking about all the things I'm grateful for. It usually starts out with my awesome mattress and comforter (my bed is like being in Heaven for me.) Also, I express my gratitude for the times when I feel physically well because I've had a lot of health issues. It's so easy to take things for granted, especially our bodies, going through our youth expecting that they will always be able to perform the way we want when we want. But, as we get older, we get the harsh wake-up call that a lot of the things we thought we could count on are not there for us as we thought they would be.

While gratitude and appreciation are very similar, I see gratitude as something that runs deeper. It's not just saying thank you when someone buys you lunch or gives you a vibrator for your birthday. It's felt more like an emotion that identifies and celebrates what you find meaningful and valuable. When someone meets a need unexpectedly or makes a sacrifice for you, the rush of emotion that comes over you is gratitude.

Positivity goes hand-in-hand with gratitude because it is nearly impossible to be truly grateful for the things, the people, and the circumstances in your life without a positive attitude. Those things aren't going to generate gratitude on their own because there are plenty of people who have more than you can imagine and still are unhappy, greedy, and ungrateful, just as there are those who have nothing and can still be joyful and express gratitude for what may seem to you like a hard situation. Gratitude comes from being able to see the gifts and the blessings in everything—even the hard and painful stuff. That only happens when you have a positive attitude and outlook.

Anywho, after what you've been through, Flower, it may be hard to feel grateful for anything; but, if you can start looking for something small, even if it's just for having sharp kitchen knives, it's a good place to start.

PARTY ALL THE TIME

If you like letting your hair down and you like to party down, go for it. Just do it in moderation. I know you may feel like you just got out of jail and all you want to do is dance and have cocktails with friends and go on dates, but this is a great time to grow and really get to know yourself again as a mature woman. You can't be doing too much of that if you have kids to take care of. I've seen women get themselves in a lot of trouble after a divorce from the consequences from parting a little too much when they are set free from the prison of their marriage. This kind of behavior can create new child custody issues if you are not being the best mom you can be for your children. If you don't have children, you are a little freer to go party; just don't get a DUI or get pregnant. That's putting yourself back in jail.

HIGHER GROUND

In my forty-five years of living and going through two divorces from the same man, as well as a few other major breakups, I've learned a few things. A few years ago, when someone asked me what were the most important things I'd learned after my divorce, I wrote these down. Look at my list and see if it inspires you, and then you can make your own list of what you've learned and what you might still need to learn.

1. *You are a fabulous flower!* It doesn't matter who likes you or hates you; as long as you like yourself, that's all that matters.

TIP: Like you so much that you don't care what anyone thinks. You could be a really great person and still not be able to control how people respond to you. Someone may not like you because you remind them of their ex, hate the way you laugh, or don't agree with something small that you said. I really do love people, but a lot of people are cray-cray, not nice, and not worth your thoughts and time. Only invest your energy in and give your heart to the good people—you know who they are.

2. *Actions speak louder than words.* Don't place too much value on what anyone says; only trust them if their actions back up their words.

TIP: If you are over thirty and believe what anyone tells you when their actions show you the opposite, it's your fault when they hurt you. If someone tells you they love you and then you catch them in the dressing room with the clerk at Nordstrom, they clearly don't understand the words coming out of their own mouth! If someone says you are the most important thing to them, and then they don't make time for you, the words mean nothing.

3. *Life is a big school.* Every single day, all the people you meet and all the places you go hold lessons for you. Pay attention!

TIP: Make eye contact and be present. Look up from your damn phone and become fully aware of your surroundings. If you see patterns emerging, whether that is in the way you keep attracting the same types of men or keep messing up in the same ways, the universe is trying to get your attention and teach you something. We are in this life to learn and grow; but, if we aren't showing up to class, we will keep repeating the same lessons.

4. *Do things that people can't take away from you.* Take classes to learn new things and explore interests you didn't make time for in the past and create opportunities to meet new people.

TIP: Your ex, a judge, or a bad fire can take all of your money or belongings at any time, but no one can take away your knowledge and experiences. Knowledge is power! Do what makes you shine. And please push yourself to try things you might not want to do or that are a bit scary. Fun, happiness, and growth can be on the other side of fear. A lot of the times I made myself go ahead with taking a class or attending an event that felt intimidating, I ended up really enjoying myself.

5. *Focus your energy and attention on the relationships that matter.* If you have children, spend every minute possible with them; they grow up so fast. If you don't have kids, spend time with your parents, siblings, or other cherished friends who love and support you.

TIP: When you have children, they need to be your number one priority at all times. If you don't have children, nurturing your relationships with your friends and family is where your focus should be. You've taken a big step in removing a toxic relationship from your life through divorce; continue that progress by purging any other relationships that don't strengthen you and help you grow—whether those are friends or family—and put your energy into deepening your connection with the people who bring positive things to your life. People come into your life to teach you things, but that doesn't always mean they are meant to stay. Learn how to identify which relationships are there for a temporary purpose and which are lasting ones and be prepared to move on from the temporary ones as you learn the lesson they have for you! But, remember to let go with as much love as you can. No need for burning bridges (or beds).

6. *Stay sexy!* This may sound harsh, but if you look at yourself in the mirror and don't want to have sex with yourself, no one else is going to want to.

TIP: Being fit and put together is really sexy, but so is confidence. But, if your confidence has been shaken by the divorce (which is understandable, especially if there was infidelity involved), you have to fake it to ya make it, pretty Flower! Let's be honest; you know how to pretend. I'm sure you've faked some orgasms in your life, so you can do this. If your body went a little south and you don't want to leave a light on when you even look at yourself, don't worry; divorce usually helps you lose some weight from the change and stress. Plus, you might get motivated to get in great shape because you want to date again.

7. *Always put life in perspective.* You realize you're dying, right? Maybe not today or tomorrow, but it could be next week. Life is too short to waste on things that don't matter in the long run and don't add to the life you're living right now.

TIP: When I really thought about the fact that I can die at any moment, I made a long list of women I know who died in their 40s and 50s, and it scared the hell out of me. Breast cancer, aneurysms, dumb accidents, etc. Most of these woman left behind children, some were very young. This realization actually made me make a bucket list. I'm so lucky I get to live in a city that has a lot to offer. Meeting interesting people, having wonderful friends, and, most important, having great children all add so much to my life. Enjoy each day you have because the only certainty in life is death. Don't waste time wallowing in sadness over something you can't change. And don't waste one day waiting for a star to fall. Put your energy into making every day a visit to Paradise City.

8. *Own your mistakes and learn from them.* Nobody is perfect, and we shouldn't be expected to be perfect; always admit when you're wrong or don't know something.

TIP: I'm not perfect, never will be, and really don't want the pressure of feeling I have to be. I usually like people because of their flaws. Of course I made mistakes in my marriage. I think it is important to admit your mistakes, treat people with kindness and respect, and follow through on commitments. I really try not to judge someone (unless they're wearing Crocs.) I admire people who can come clean and say, "I fucked up. I don't know if I can make it right, but I want to try." I trust those people. You are going to make mistakes, and that's okay. How else do you learn if you don't mess up once in a while? The people who blame others for everything are the ones you run from. I ask every divorced person I encounter what their part was in the failed marriage, and if they're dancing in the dark and can't come up with an answer, that tells me they have not been honest with themselves and they are likely to repeat the same mistakes.

9. *Keep it real!* Find what is really important to you, evaluate your values, and live by those standards, not anyone else's.

TIP: No matter how much money I have or how successful I get, for me, my success is raising my two boys alone without a washer or dryer. There are a lot of the comforts of life I've had to sacrifice since getting divorced. When I was younger I thought those things mattered. They really don't. Having my family's basic needs met and money for some nice shoes once in a while is enough. The only time I get a bit envious of anyone is when they tell me they have their own washer or dryer. If you don't know what your values are, look at your bank account and see where you are spending your mony mony, and that will give you a clue. Then look at where you spend your time and who you spend it with. If you don't like the picture this paints, start making changes.

10. *Read and learn.* Being alone again is a perfect time to make changes to better yourself. Do something each day to expand your mind.

TIP: I've read about 300 books in the last five years. I love to read and learn about new things. I actually find it really exciting when I've been thinking I know something and then discover I'm really wrong. Having to look at something differently is a great way to open up your mind and become a better, stronger, more appealing person. I missed out on a lot of learning opportunities growing up due to some hearing and vision problems, so I don't take it for granted. Even if you hate reading or your eyes are still too puffy and swollen from all the tears to see, try to read a little something every day. Did you know most of the life lessons you need to know can be found in Dr. Seuss books? Dr. Seuss books are all about being yourself, persevering, finding appreciation, achieving balance, being creative, showing love and friendship, and so much more. This is one of my favorite quotes: "With your head full of brains and your shoes full of feet, you're too smart to go down any not so good street."—Dr. Seuss

11. *The only connection you need is the one with your higher power."*

Find your higher power and focus on that connection every day because it's the only one you really have.

TIP: God as we come to understand him or her is an important and powerful part of getting through the hard times in life and moving toward better things. God hooks me up all the time because I pray all the time. When bad things happen, my prayer usually starts out with, *God, what the hell?* Family, friends, kids, and romantic relationships will come and go; but, when you have a really strong connection to a higher power that feels real in your life and challenges you to always do and be better, you won't have a break down when things come and go. Of course, you will be hurt, but you'll be so grounded in your faith you won't become a fallen angel.

12. *Shut up: Really listen to people.* You can't learn anything from anyone if your mind chatter is out of control and you think your thoughts are more important.

TIP: I'm really friendly and find it really easy to strike up a conversation with anyone wherever I go. When I interact with someone, I usually start with a compliment to get things started and end up in a conversation. I used to have a bunch of mind chatter going on trying to prepare what to say next, and I used to miss out being fully present for what that amazing person had to say. If you are so focused on getting a clever or intelligent response ready before they've said anything, you are likely to end up looking foolish and stupid because you aren't responding to what they actually said. I've learned to really listen to others and shut the hell up. It makes for much better conversation.

13. *Don't tell your story.* Let others talk and just listen. Don't try to fix, one-up, or distract them from their pain.

TIP: I used to think I was helping someone by telling them my story when they told me something awful that happened to them. I thought by sharing my experience that it helped them, but sometimes it really doesn't. I realized that sometimes I was topping or dismissing their story, as if my pain was more important or worse than their pain. I didn't realize how inappropriate that was until I really thought about it, and people did it to me a few times when I needed things to be about me. As far as I know, they don't give out suffering awards, so you never need to be in competition. Bad stuff happens to everyone and if your friend is suffering, there is a valuable lesson brewing for her to learn. If she asks you, of course share; listening to others does help sometimes, but don't do it without an invitation. The best way you can be there for them is to just be there.

14. *Trust your instincts.* It's so easy; just trust that little fabulous voice inside of you that is gentle and kind.

TIP: I have to believe that there is some sort of plan for my life and that I'm being led to good things. I wouldn't have all these great desires and all night passions if they were not going anywhere or weren't valuable to my growth process. I used to try to make things happen, but that only led me to failure. Things happen when the time is right, people show up when the time is right, and people leave at the right time too. Typically, you are not going to get a red flashing sign shouting the answers to your questions. We don't always know what we are supposed to do or how to act, but clarity will come with trust and patience. You can't hurry love and you can't force wisdom and knowledge.

15. *NO!* The best word you can learn to say is NO, and be able to say it without an explanation.

TIP: You don't ever owe anyone an explanation. Don't ever let anyone pressure you to explain yourself. This doesn't mean you have a license to be a bitch. Be gracious when someone asks you to explain, but stay firm with your NO. If you try to explain, they are going to argue with you anyway, so don't do that to yourself. You are fully entitled to decide what you do and don't want to do and should only change your mind if you decide, upon further consideration that it is worth doing. Don't just take it from me. The seventy-year-old actress Helen Mirren told the *New York Daily News* that she regrets not telling more people to "Fuck off" in her life. I think we should all learn from that and not be so accommodating sometimes. Especially, when people are disrespectful by pushing their desires on us.

16. *I hate sushi.* It's okay to hate sushi ... or whatever the hell you hate.

TIP: All my friends love sushi, and it seems like every single person in LA loves sushi except me. I'm never going to eat it, and I don't understand why anyone would want to eat raw fish (or even a California roll), and I don't get the appeal of eating something that most people admit has given them food poisoning at some point. I like my food cooked; it's just who I am. The point is, don't let anyone make you feel inferior for your tastes. You are a unique, individual person who gets to have unique, individual desires, interests, and likes. Own that and celebrate it, Flower. It's who you are!

WAIT

Wait. This is what you've been waiting for—the chance to love you! I'm only going to say this one time: there are many benefits to being single if you are willing to accept this as the reality of your situation and allow yourself to make the most of it. The list can go on and on and on, but here are my Top Ten reasons I enjoy being single:

1. You can have cereal or a glass of wine for dinner;
2. You get to sleep in a big bed without anyone taking the covers or crowding you;
3. You can leave your clothes lying around;
4. You don't have to tell anyone where you're going;
5. You can indulge yourself with $500 shoes, and no one is there to tell you no;
6. You can walk around naked without anyone groping at you;
7. You get to play DJ and blast your 80s music;
8. You get to control the remote and watch the shows you want;
9. You don't have to shift your schedule to accommodate someone else;
10. You can travel where you want to go and have your own adventures.

Whether you wanted the divorce or not, you are now single. Enjoy it because you really don't have another option. I know some people hate being alone; but, if you want to find love again, you need to be alone for a while to heal and get to know yourself again first. My list is mostly fun ways to look at being alone in a positive way, but there are many ways you can really evolve into an amazing and empowered person while you cool your jets and wait for the signs that you are completely ready to get back out there. Just don't do what Laura did.

THINK OF LAURA

Laura was a tall, thin, very pretty doctor. But, she stayed home a lot because she didn't like to go out to eat alone, go to the movies alone, or go on vacation alone. She had the money to go out to really nice places, yet chose to stay home with bad takeout and Netflix. I talked with her one day and told her about all the things I do by myself because I'm single, three of my good friends got divorced and moved out of state, and my oldest son left for college. I have to eat alone sometimes and I don't really eat fast food, so that means going to restaurants alone. I usually take my computer or a book, but I often end up meeting someone interesting to talk to. I have no problem going to a movie alone; people do it all the time, and you aren't supposed to talk to someone during a movie anyway, so it shouldn't be a big deal. Vacations can be really fun alone if you treat it like an adventure. I've never been on a solo vacation when I didn't meet someone fun to hang out with. But, Laura just didn't want to do it; she felt pathetic going places by herself. That thinking was keeping her from possibly meeting the man she was hoping to save her from being alone. Some mold spores will grow spontaneously in your apartment, but men don't. You have to expand your world if you want to have new people in it.

PERSONAL JESUS

As most know, Jesus was a great carpenter. I felt one with him when I successfully put my children's bunk beds together after we moved into our apartment. Before that, the only thing that I successfully put together in my life was a puzzle. Yes, I had to Google what all the tools were and how they worked. I got a few bruises and broke some nails; but, I did it, and now I can fix most things myself ... except my son's basketball hoop. I don't like to admit defeat, but I almost poured gasoline on it and lit it on fire in the street!

My point is this: you will learn how to do things on your own that are amazing skills to have. Sure, it's nice when you don't have to do some things for yourself, but knowing you can if you choose will make you feel like a rockstar ... or

Jesus. Don't be upset if you don't know how to change a light
bulb or fix the toilet. Use this opportunity to learn. Obviously,
some tasks still need the help of a skilled professional, but pay
attention to what they do and learn from him (or her). Don't
ever let anyone come and fix something without teaching you
how to do it. Most handy men will be just thrilled to teach a
pretty Flower how to fix something. They don't need to know
they are putting themselves out of business in the process!
The more you learn to do for yourself, the more confident
you will be when you get out and start meeting new people.

I'LL BE THERE FOR YOU

No, I'm not talking about the *Friends* theme song; I'm referring
to Bon Jovi's hit, though both have the same sentiment. These
five words, "I'll be there for you," are hard to come by. But, I
swear to you, your friendships are really important as you go
through transition. Surround yourself with people who are
loving and kind and will have your back. I have a theory that
we all are born with three circle groups: First is the circle of
your close peeps—you tell them everything, the good, the
bad, and the ugly, and they love you even though you are
messed up—and if you have more than 2-3 of them you can
count yourself lucky. The second circle is where most people
in your life will fall—the people you really like, but they are
only exposed to the good in your life—who are part of your
social circle but will never be in the inner sanctum of your
world. The third circle includes the people who are casual
acquaintances—maybe colleagues, a boss, neighbors, etc.
who don't know a whole lot more about you than is on your
resume or social media profile—and while you may hang out
with them once in a while, they are basically kept at arm's
length.

I know it seems odd to compartmentalize relationships
like this, but it is necessary. As you get older and your
interactions with people get more complex, you will see why

I am right. You will always wish you didn't tell the girl at work something about you because odds are good that she will either use it to get that promotion over you or it will get blabbed at the company Christmas party after too much eggnog.

Finding first circle friends is hard, and it can take years. When you do find one, love the hell out of them and always be there for them! Most of the time they will outlast any romantic relationship you have. With a breakup/divorce you are kicking someone close out of your first circle group, and that's why it's so difficult to do. You let them close to you and now they probably won't even get to go in the third circle group. This is why pulling your other first circle friends close is so important when you are going through this transition.

FRIENDS
Before we go any further let's talk about friends. How many of us have a lot of them? If you want to be the girlfriend that everyone likes and wants to hang out with, here are some tips that will help you as you are trying to cultivate new friendships. You don't need to follow all of them but keep these things in mind.

1. Always say less than you think—choose your words carefully and be respectful when you do express your opinions. Yeah, I have trouble with this one.
2. Don't make promises you can't keep. Always keep your word and follow through on the things you commit to.
3. Always say a kind word to someone, but only if you really mean it.
4. Be interested in others' lives. This one is hard in our self-absorbed culture.
5. Be positive. Don't dwell on your sicknesses or disappointments.

6. Don't gossip! It's mean and hurtful.

MODERN DAY COWBOY

We've all seen the show *Modern Family* that demonstrates how the stereotypical *Leave it to Beaver* family is not the norm anymore. We are in a no man's land as family structures are being redefined. It's no longer just a male husband, female wife, one boy, one girl, and a Golden Retriever. I've seen men in "wife roles" and females in "husband roles." The taboos around single parenthood are disappearing, and the stigma of adoption is nearly gone. Whether you have two husbands having a child through a surrogate or two wives with a sperm donor, conception is breaking all the rules these days. There are many situations where grandparents, friends, and foster families are raising children whose parents can't be there for whatever reason.

Your family is perfect just the way it is now! Whether it's just you and a cat, or you had to move into your sister's crazy household, it is what it is. Love it and embrace it because it's what you've got. You can waste your time sitting around thinking you had a better family, but it's simply a waste of time. Your family is what you make it. It will be dysfunctional if you let drama rule your relationships. It will be a safe haven if you embrace each other with love.

ALONE

Do I hear the ticking of your clock? It's probably shouting at you that if you don't get pregnant soon you'll end up in the dark. That's just a stupid reason to start dating quickly after a divorce. All that will get you is another divorce and a child who doesn't deserve to be caught in the middle.

Lots of women are choosing to have babies on their own now, without waiting to involve a husband or partner. My entertainment attorney, my cousin, and several other women I know, did it this way and saved themselves and their children so much pain. Yes, the challenges of single parenthood are still there, but at least you are going into that scenario with your eyes open, knowing it's all on you. When you marry and have kids, you are expecting to have a partner, and when that doesn't happen, you feel blindsided and lost. You also don't have the agony of a broken heart and the nightmare of an ex who may fight you every step of the way.

Choosing to have a baby on your own may not be what you want to do or dreamed you would do, but know it is an option, and definitely a better one than rushing into a new relationship just to quiet your raging hormones. In my opinion, having babies on your own is the way to go! If your husband leaves, you don't have to put little kids through hell of going back and forth between parents, and you don't have to go to court! I'm beyond jealous of my friends and family who had babies on their own. I've been through hell and back with child support and visitation issues. I would've spent the same amount of time and money raising a child on my own and not had any of the headache and heartache. I know a lot of my friends with cray-cray ex-husbands that feel the same way. Single ladies, you can do this on your own! If you get married, you have a 50/50 shot that you will be doing it on your own anyway. I didn't make the rule. It is what it is!

FYI, I have a friend who had a baby on her own and one year later met the man of her dreams. They got married and he loves her son.

JUMP

Go ahead and jump. You may be thinking, *Annette, I feel like I've been flying without a parachute for this whole time. Why would I want to take more risk?* The thing is, it's really healthy to feel uncomfortable and get out of your comfort zone, and there's probably no better time than when your world has already been turned upside down because you aren't settled into being complacent and in a routine. It will be easier to take bold steps when you're already in motion.

Make a list of activities or places you haven't explored with in 100 miles of where you live and do something new each week. I suggest going alone. Take some time to be dependent only on yourself for fun and pleasure. Finding contentment in yourself leads to all sorts of exciting self-discovery and opportunities to become the best version of you possible. It may feel awkward at first, but in time you won't care at all.

ON MY OWN

No one said it would be easy, but if you embrace your time in this uncharted territory, it's the best opportunity to change your life for the better! Don't be afraid to be alone, be more afraid of being with someone who makes you feel alone. Taking some time to love the hell out of yourself after this difficult transition is the way to go.

I like eating alone. I like going for walks alone. I like going to the movies alone. I like exercising alone. I like going on vacation alone. Learn to like being alone because you have to live with you. I like me and I make me laugh all the time, sometime others don't do that! Learn to like you so much that spending time with yourself is even more enjoyable than being with others. If you are the best company you keep, it will help when you do try to meet new people. FYI, I do want to find a guy at some point and fall in love again, but I'm in the best spot ever. I won't settle because I'm perfectly happy alone.

Until you really love you, you can't attract a really healthy individual for your next husband/wife. Remember that! You can't attract good healthy friends either. This might be a great time to get rid of some friends that aren't acting in your best interests. You know who they are.

AIN'T NOBODY

Ain't nobody gonna love you better than you will love yourself. Be super kind and loving to yourself and take it one day at a time. Live each day like it may be your last day on the planet. You will get through this hard time, learn, and find a ton of happiness. I've talked to so many women who use this time to work on themselves and fall in love with themselves, and their lives always ends up full of love, joy, and happiness again. Deep heartbreak tends to humble us as we hit rock bottom. Years later, we all see why it happened, and most of us are truly grateful for the experience. I know when it's happening you can't see that at all, so just keep it in the back of your mind for now. Enjoy your life, have fun, and *wang chung* ... I still don't know what that means.

Chapter 8
I'M COMING OUT

If you want the world to know that you're coming out, you will have to have an online dating profile so you can let them know. I'm just going to lightly touch on this crazy little dating game that is played in 2018. If you are going to start dating, you need to read my book *Don't Go in that Room!*. No, it's not a shameless plug; my book will explain in more detail why I'm telling you not to do certain things here. Please read several dating books before you date, not just mine. I list the good ones in my other book. There are some really bad dating advice books out there with really bad suggestions such as male coaches telling you to ask men out, to split the check, and that it's okay to have sex after a few dates. Please consider the source on that advice and read the good ones. Women should all get together and have a bon fire for those stupid books that are not empowering for women.

My advice is for those who want to find true love, to be treated properly, and to find a commitment again with the right man for them. If you're looking for a one-night stand or don't mind getting screwed over and spending way too much time crying, my advice isn't for you. Some critics of my dating book stated that my advice is old-fashioned; and they are right! I believe in the old-fashioned rules where guys have to treat women with love and respect. Today's dating methods are not working since so many women are single and can't find a good man.

MIXED UP WORLD
The dating world today is all mixed up. It isn't like it was in the 80s when friends used to introduce you to their friends, parties were great places to meet each other, and the bar

was a safer place to meet men. It's rare to meet someone IRL (in real life) these days. Dating happens online and it's a million men playing a numbers game. You may feel special when a guy clicks like on your photo or made you one of his favorites, but who knows how many other pretty Flowers he's done that to. I've had guys tell me they do that to a ton of pretty girls to see who responds, and then go out with all of the girls who responded.

You can't fall for a man quickly or think you're special until he proves it by taking you out on numerous dates and begins to make a special place for you in his life, otherwise you're setting yourself up for pain that you don't have time for. I'm sorry to say, but you're probably a number until he shows you by his actions that you are not, and if his actions are like an octopus all over your breasts and lady center, that doesn't mean he really likes you; that only means he likes you enough to fuck you.

Asking about your likes and needs and then meeting them through his actions, wanting to meet your family and children, and learn all the stupid little things about you— this is what's important. I had a guy tell me he knew he was falling for me when he saw how I eat toast and found it endearing. I put my toast in the freezer before I put my chunky peanut butter on it. I hate melted peanut butter. Also, I prefer the end piece that nobody likes. I'd set the timer on the microwave for five minutes and sit on the counter with my coffee waiting for my toast to cool. You never know when one of your quirks is the thing that's going to make you stand out to him. It's the real moments that usually make him fall in love, not the sex.

HIT ME WITH YOUR BEST SHOT

So, you think you're a real tough cookie, but the modern dating scene is pretty tough too, and if you're just getting back into it after twenty years of marriage, you are in for a really rude awakening. If someone is not fighting fair, that's okay, you won't care, if your self-esteem is really high. The most important thing you need before you start dating is confidence. Confidence is sexy and it's a power we all have, or can learn to have. If you are not ready to go out there knowing how amazing you are, you're not ready to date!

Here are five more traits you need to have before you start dating. If you already have all these things, get out there and strut your fabulous self around; if you have one or two areas to work on, get working on them—life is short. If you were going to keep taking shit you would have stayed with your ex, so don't go into dating without being ready to fight for yourself.

1. *She's a Bad Mama Jama* - You have to be a badass. Really know who you are and love yourself so much that any bad behavior from men hits your armor and never touches you.

2. *Private Eyes (They're Watching You)* - You have to be a detective. Get your BS detector working at 100 percent. Don't take anything a man tells you at face value. Trust but verify. Make sure words are supported by actions.

3. *Self-Control* - You have to be strong sexually. It's going to be tempting if it's been awhile, but don't give in to sex too early with a man if you want a relationship. Control your lady center and know how valuable it is to men.

4. *Walk Like an Egyptian* - You have to be able to walk away at any time. Be willing and prepared to walk away if you are disrespected. This is your second chance at love, so don't tolerate unacceptable behavior for even a minute.

5. *Wanted Man* - You have to get what you want first. Think about your needs in the relationship first, not

his, because he isn't going to put yours first. What do you need and want from this relationship? What are you willing to do to get it?

THRILLER

It's your first date in a long time and you may feel like horror is looking you right between the eyes. Your single friends might have shared with you their pain and agony around trying to find a healthy, stable, compatible person who lacks fetishes or addictions, but it's another thing to experience it yourself.

If you're divorced with kids, you know that you have some baggage now, and the guy you are going to be with will have some too. A lot of older recently divorced men don't want to get married again. They want to play the field and have lots of sex with difference women. They almost seem to be making up for lost time and have zero intention of getting close to anyone ever again, or more importantly to them losing any more money.

Online dating is essentially dating a bunch of people at the same time. Guys will try to make moves on you while they are still making moves on other women. Just note, as long as his online profile is active, he's still open to possibilities with other women, and just because that one profile he met you on is down, it doesn't mean that he's not on a few more you don't know about. Be a smart Flower!

But, online dating has worked for numerous people, so if you have the time and energy to weed through a ton of profiles, go ahead and have as much fun with it as you can! But, watch your expectations going into online dating. To get to your Richie Sambora, you will have to sort through a lot of men with bad long hair. I don't know anyone who said they actually enjoyed the online dating process. They enjoyed meeting their husband or wife if they met online, but not the dating process.

I have to throw in my five favorite dates over the years to show you examples of dating. You get all dressed up with the hope of finding that special man that makes your heart smile and you get this.

MY FAVORITE MEN WHO GOT ONE DATE . . . LOL!

The Masturbator – The short version of this long story is that I walked in on him masturbating during our date! I jumped and spilled an entire cup of water down my shirt. I had to drive an hour home in the car with him after that happened. The kicker was he asked me if I had a good time on the way home! This was the first time in my life that I've *ever* been at a loss for words! I seriously couldn't get a word out ... nothing, not even a squeak! Maybe I should've taken this as a compliment?

The Checker - He interviewed me, and every time I answered a question to his liking, he made a check in the air with his finger. If I answered the question "wrong" he pouted his lip. Poor guy wanted a wife that skies. He was devastated when I said that I don't ski. No check in the air for me! I grabbed my bag to leave, but he said I would get more checks, he was sure of it! Of course, I had to stick around and see if I would get more checks, so I ordered a second glass of wine. Then he told me he doesn't want a wife that drinks too much and pouted his lip.

The Food Line - I hate when people eat off my plate! I don't know if this is an issue for most, but it's an issue for me and it freaks me out! Eat your own damn food; I don't know you yet! I understand that it was $25 chocolate pudding in Beverly Hills, but don't put your freaking fork in my pudding! There are 400 different types of bacteria in the mouth. I tried to explain what he did when he asked me why I wasn't eating my pudding but he wasn't getting it. After I went off about it, I think he learned to keep his fork to himself on a first date!

The Meat Guy - This guy told me how much he liked meat ... for an hour! Nope, he wasn't a butcher, just a guy who really liked meat! It was like having a date with the beef version of Bubba in Forrest Gump. *T-Bone Steak, Sirloin Steak, Top Loin Steak, Round Steak, Porterhouse Steak, Flat Bone Sirloin Steak, Rib Steak, Rib Eye Steak* ... just kill me! Thank God I'm not a vegetarian, although he didn't even ask. I almost told him I was just to see his reaction, but I was afraid I may get an hour lecture on how my body needs protein.

The Proposal – On our first date he planned our home and wedding. I did get a pole dance room in the new house, which was very thoughtful of him! I love thoughtful men! I really want a pole dance room. I have to throw this in for kicks ... I asked him why he got divorced, he told me he cheated on his wife because she was a 4 emotionally, but a 10 in bed, and the woman he cheated on her was a 4 in bed, and a 10 emotionally. I don't date men who cheated on their wives. In fact, I ask on the first date and tell them not to see me again if they cheated. Obviously, I didn't even have to ask this dumb ass; he came right out with numerical values comparing his mistress and wife.

All of these men were dates set up by friends except the masturbator; I met him online. You have to remember to keep your sense of humor in dating and laugh at this stuff.

DON'T YOU WANT ME
Baby, don't you want me? Even if you are in shape, beautiful, have a great job working as a waitress in a cocktail bar, and are low on baggage, you will still get rejected once in a while. Always remember, "Rejection is Protection." When you're rejected online or IRL, it is you, but it's not you. There can

be a million different reasons they don't feel a connection, so don't ever take it personally. You reject people as well for different reasons. It could be because you have a dog or cat, like the beach, don't ski ... who the hell knows? Just don't let it discourage you.

Finding the right person who matches up with you is not easy! It takes time to find your second/third husband or wife, and this time the pressure is on to make a better decision.

If you've done the necessary work on yourself, made your list of priorities to know what type of man matches with you, and waited a sufficient period of time before jumping back into the game of love, you will find a good partner. If you go on a few dates and you feel rejected or not good enough STOP dating! Work on yourself for another few months; your emotions will let you know where you are at during the dating process.

THE FINAL COUNTDOWN

These are the dating rules I suggest that work like butter if you want to be heading for Venus. Never spend one minute longer than necessary with someone who isn't treating you the way you want to be treated! I know it's hard when you like someone and have to say *goodbye to you*, but it's so much easier to do it within the first month of dating, instead of after a year.

So, here it is, it's the final countdown:

1. *The Chase.* Drop the handkerchief so to speak by clicking like on his photo or make eye contact and smile IRL. Let men chase you; they will if they like you. You're a flower; you don't chase men. EVER! If he sees your profile online and thinks you're worth pursuing, he will get in touch with you! If you do the asking, he may just go out with you to be polite because he's a nice guy, but it

won't be because he really likes you. If he didn't like you enough to ask you out first it's not because he's shy; it's because he's not that interested.

2. *Dirty Diana.* If you are looking for love, please don't give a man your lady center until you know he is worthy of it. After three months of dating is my rule of thumb. Sounds too long? I actually think women should start considering waiting until they get an engagement ring in this crazy online dating world if they don't want to get used. You really have to know someone before you sleep with them. He could be on tons of dating sites and sleeping with a lot of women. And these days, one out of four people have an STD. He could sleep with you, never call again, but you are stuck with his presence anyway because of his lovely parting gift of herpes or HPV.

3. *Meet Me Halfway.* I'm sure Mr. Kenny Loggins knows that you shouldn't ever ask a woman to meet halfway. He just sang this great song. *Don't ever meet half way on a first date; men should come to you.* Pick a place close to your house. If he's not willing to be chivalrous on the first date when he is trying to win you over, how's he going to act later on after you've had sex with him or have been dating for a few months?. Men should be hunting you down! Besides, unless he is way too obsessed with his own appearance, it's going to take you longer to get ready. You have to look pretty for the date; they just have to show up. Remember, when a woman comes a little too easy to a man, they don't want her. They like the girl who is a challenge. He perceives her as high value. Plus, you don't have time to be driving anywhere if you have kids at home, and he shouldn't ask you too!

4. *Proud Mary.* Always be a classy, high-value woman. If a man asks you for suggestions for the date, please give him

three choices of things you like to do in your area that are free or really inexpensive. You shouldn't have dinner or drinks on a first date if you've never met the person. You don't want to end up stuck in a restaurant for two hours with someone you don't have chemistry with. If you go to a museum on a free day, a shopping center, or beach and take a walk, you can really get to know someone and you can leave when you want, you don't have to wait for food or a check. And you don't have to feel bad that he bought you dinner and you know you're never going to see him again. This is a meet and greet if you met online, and you should only give them an hour or so. If you really connect, go ahead and hang out longer, but just make sure you end the date! Ending the date first makes them want more of you!

5. *Misery and Gin.* Don't drink at a meet and greet. Do you go to a job interview and drink? No, you do not, unless you're an alcoholic! You are looking for a second husband or a good man to spend your time with if you're reading this book; do you want to make that decision not fully present? I don't think so. You don't want to get divorced again! Make sober decisions. You can't afford to get divorced again emotionally or financially. Getting buzzed on a date with a stranger can lead to so many horrible consequences. There will be time for enjoying a glass of wine on a nice dinner if the meet and greet goes well. But, first impressions are really important and are hard to reverse, so make sure you are as clear-headed as you can be and put your best self out there.

6. *Better Be Good to Me.* Men should pay for the date if they ask you out. Men used to hunt and kill things (and some still do) and bring them home to their mates to provide for them. It's instinctual even today, so let them! You can tell how much a man likes you from what he is willing

to invest in you. Men spend money on women they like. This is a good litmus test.

Allowing someone to take care of you a little is not cause for revoking your feminist card. Feminism is about recognizing your own power as a woman and not allowing someone to treat you poorly and try to give you less than you're worth. And, I'm not suggesting you become a kept woman who just takes and takes and takes. This is about relationship and partnership. If a man is investing in you, you must do nice things for the man who is courting you properly. Learn their love language. What makes them feel loved? You have to reciprocate with the things you have to offer.

Exception to the Rule: If you're an alpha female and decide to ask a man out, then you should pay for the date. If you want to take care of a man, there is nothing wrong with finding a passive man who brings most of the feminine energy to the relationship and who likes to be taken care of. Go ahead, pay for dinner, open his door, give him a sweater if he's cold, etc. Just don't complain about the role you chose later on. I can't count the number of women who tell me they are feminists and think that everything should be split, but then cry to me when they aren't getting treated well and that they have to do everything.

Most women want to be swept off their feet and romanced, yet they still cut a man off at the knees when he tries to do the things he instinctively equates with romance, and then cry that chivalry is dead. STOP THE MADNESS. It's okay to be pampered. You deserve it. You're a flower. It's not about the fucking money, it's about romance—feeling special and appreciated. It's about letting him use the tools he has in his toolbox to show you his love.

Here's another thing to consider: Dating can be very

expensive for females—the time and money you invest in getting your makeup, hair, nails, clothes, and physique where they have to be to attract men. If you have little kids at home after your divorce, you may even have to pay for a babysitter, and that can run you $60 for about three hours. So, it's not that you aren't spending and investing in him. He just reaps the benefits in a different way.

7. *Material Girl* - As we just established, men are going to want to spend money on a woman they are interested in. They are going to want to impress you and spoil you. That's normal and it's fine. But, don't order anything expensive when you go out on the real dinner date, and don't drink on the first few dates! I'm really against drinking and dating! Get to know someone with all your senses working at 100 percent. You can't afford to make a mistake at this point in your life, and alcohol will cloud your judgement! It's not very appropriate to have a man spend any money on you, if you don't think the relationship has potential. Be very respectful of yourself and him, and be a high-value woman at all times. Don't treat his invitation as a meal ticket. Don't turn his affection for you into a way to cash in while you can. Men have complained to me lately that women use them for dinner, I personally don't know any women who would ever consider doing that, but I guess this happens. You don't need me to tell you how tacky and classless that is. I think it's more of a rumor by men who took a woman out to dinner, but she never saw him again because she didn't like him, and he feels used. He'd rather think she used him for dinner instead of being honest with himself that she just didn't like him.

This "who is going to pay the check" issue is out of hand, and doesn't need to be. If a man asks you out, he pays. You say no if you don't like him, you say yes if you do and it's okay to take what he gives you. End of story. Men and women are different, contrary to what some people want to believe—we don't get equal pay, men can't have babies, women have way more to risk, and we bond differently during sexual intercourse. I'm certainly not saying we are less than; I'm saying we are different than men. A dog can't be a cat and a cat can't be a dog. If you don't like those facts, there are operations that can change you into a different gender; and, with all the new stem-cell research, who knows, we will probably be able to grow you a penis in time.

8. *Leave It* - Recognize and accept when he's not into you. If a man isn't chasing you or is acting like he could take you or leave you ... run! This man is not worth your time. Watch his words and actions. If he tells you he likes or loves you but doesn't make plans to see you and go out of his way for you, he's lying or doesn't know how to love. Words and actions always line up. Always! A man in love wants to spend every minute with you. Why sign up to be miserable and feel lonely and unloved just like you did in your marriage? Always remember that one guy you didn't like who that was in love with you and how it felt when you couldn't get rid of him. That's how it feels like when a guy likes you. If your guy isn't begging for the next chance to see you before you've finished the date you're on, he only sees you as an option.

9. *PacMan Fever* - Don't ever play games! It's so childish and a waste of time to play games and try to manipulate someone you are dating. You're already divorced and have been through a lot. You don't have time for this shit! If a man likes you he will jump from a plane and fight a lion for you; no games will be necessary. If he's playing games with texts or phone calls, he's just not that

interested or 53 going on 12. You know when a man likes you; they don't leave you alone. If you're not sure he likes you, he doesn't. Whether you are listening to advice that teaches you to string him along and breadcrumb him to get him interested, or he's the one doing that to you, it is a cruel way to treat people and it never gets you the desired result. There is a dance that happens when you are getting to know someone that involves not being too available or overeager, but there is a way to do that with self-respect and dignity and show kindness to them.

10. *Lying Excuses* - Don't make those damn excuses for him! Especially if he isn't making them for himself! If you have to make excuses of any sort pertaining to why he didn't call you when he said he would, or why he cancelled the date last minute, or why he's not committing to you, or when the relationship has progressed, why you're not included in the Facebook pictures, or why you haven't met the family or friends, he's not into you nearly as much as you are telling yourself he is. Sure he may like you and like having you around, but a guy who doesn't want to lose you will make damned sure he does everything he can to lock you down. If you're making excuses, get therapy! Don't make excuses for anyone, EVER.

There are so many good men out there, and you will find them if you are being the best person you can be. The good men will flock to you because like attracts like! Follow these rules and you will be on your way to finding the right kind of relationship for you.

SAFETY DANCE

You can dance with men if you want to, but it will not lead to anything positive right now. It would be so much better to masturbate until you find someone worth the access you are giving them. In other words, have sex with someone you love ... YOU! You need sex; we all do. It's natural and normal to want sex, and if you don't have a partner you have to do what you need to do. Nope, nobody likes to talk about masturbation; but, do yourself a favor and order a toy online or go to your local sex shop. I guarantee there is one somewhere near you. Ask the salesgirl for help, and if you're embarrassed, tell her you're getting it for your friend! She'll know you're lying but it's all good.

Besides, the first time you sleep with a man it's usually awkward, they cum too fast and you don't have an orgasm. If you're part of the 50 percent of women who can't having an orgasm though vaginal intercourse, why put your emotions and health at risk over unfulfilling intercourse? Especially if you have children at home that you have to take care. FYI, I know three women who had sex with a man early on and got herpes. These men left them after they got the sex. Now, for the rest of their lives they have to suffer and tell men that they have herpes before they have sex with them. Giving your lady center away quickly would simply be stupid and you're not a stupid Flower.

WE DON'T HAVE TO TAKE OUR CLOTHES OFF

You shouldn't be taking your clothes off and having a good time with someone while you're still recovering from divorce, especially if you want a relationship. You need time to heal, and guys also need to heal from their own failed relationships, but they shouldn't be doing their healing in your lady center! Be supportive and build a friendship while they are getting themselves ready for a relationship. Since you went through a divorce, it's your duty to help others going through one. But, if you are developing feelings, you simply need to take a step back. You don't need to take your clothes off with this guy to have a good time! Enjoy each other in non-sexual ways until you're both ready for a relationship that is healthy, loving, and kind. A man who wants a real relationship and sees you as a high-value woman doesn't leave and will wait for the sex.

OH, SHEILA

Oh, Sheila, what were you thinking? She started sleeping with a very recently divorced man several months after her own divorce. She told herself she wasn't looking for anything serious, and he was really chasing her. After ten weeks she gave in and had sex with him. Of course, she started to have feelings for him and he started to lose feelings for her. I see this all the time. Women go in thinking they can have sex and not get hurt. If you are the rare woman who doesn't bond during sex, perhaps it's time to seek professional help or at least find out what planet you're from. But, for the rest of us, sex inevitably leads to a deeper connection with someone, and if they aren't ready to make that connection it can result in some reactions that can be quite painful.

Sheila knew he was recently divorced and still hurting, but she went and did it anyway. She was really hurt when he didn't want to be with her anymore, and told her he wasn't ready for a relationship. I couldn't feel all that bad for her, because she knew where he was at and did it anyway. Don't make the same mistake because you are just setting yourself up for heartache. And haven't you already had enough of that?

LITTLE JEANNE

Little Jeanne was recently divorced and started dating again. She was dating a man for four months who had two small children. Jeanne didn't have children. This guy called her and texted her every day, gave her cute pet names and always made her feel special. But, when they did have a date it was usually something free—he would get her to make him dinner at her apartment, he might pick up some take out, or have her do it. He used his kids as excuses all the time if he had to cancel or didn't call.

He invited her away for a weekend, and somehow he forgot cash and his bank card. She had to pay for everything, including the hotel room. On the last day of the trip he was acting odd and said he needed to rush back home.

She didn't hear from him for a few days, so she texted him. He responded, but something was really off. She sent him a text telling him the cost of the trip and asked if he was going to pay her back. He waited a few days and paid half the bill. She never heard from him again. He actually blocked her. She tried to call him and it went right to voicemail. She decided to try calling him from her friend's phone right after. It rang and, you guessed it, he picked right up. This is what we call ghosting! Some men will date you for a few months and just disappear instead of being a man and telling you to your face that he isn't interested in pursuing the relationship.

Ghosting hurts because you have no idea why they just left and you gave them your heart (and probably your body). It's a disgusting feeling of being used and discarded like a piece of trash. This is another example of why you don't sleep with men quickly. Are you seeing why three months of dating isn't even long enough nowadays?

KISS ME DEADLY
Kissing once or twice on the first few dates isn't deadly, but, having sex once or twice can be. Men and women both bond through sex, but it's more like this: Women release oxytocin, which is like Krazy® Glue. It's toxic and not safe to use around children. God forbid you get it on your hands; you will get stuck forever. It's made to really keep shit together. Men, on the other hand, release dopamine, which is like the Elmer's® glue kids use in a kindergarten class and get all

over there little fingers. It's safe, non-toxic, doesn't stick all that well, but enough for it to keep the macaroni and sequins stuck to their artwork for a little while.

I see women making this mistake all the time after a divorce—they're lonely, so they start dating too soon and sleep with the wrong man. Women need to fully understand that their lady center doesn't know the difference between sex with a good man or bad man, it just knows the size of the penis and can feel the oxytocin released. When that happens, voilà, Krazy glue attachment to the wrong guy who screws her over after he gets the sex. Don't do this, pretty Flower. Learn from other women's mistakes anytime you can. If you need to learn this lesson for yourself, I just hope you can get through it without getting an STD or pregnancy to make things worse, and you can move on and never repeat the mistake.

I've had several men on first dates tell me that they slept with their long-term girlfriends on the first date, hinting that if I sleep with them we also could have a relationship. I tell them they won't be sleeping with me without an STD check, three months of dating, and courting me properly. Always be a high value woman if you're looking for a good man who wants a relationship and love! If all women set this standard with men, dating would be easy. But, we all have that one friend with low self-esteem who lets men use them for sex and treat them poorly. Don't be one of those women. It's seriously your choice how you want to be treated. If he walks away because you won't have sex, thank God you protected yourself and made a wise choice because that is clearly all he was after.

Listen, I'm all for sex and having a lot of it when you find the right man. I believe in treating a man lovingly and with kindness when he is treating you well. I'm all for throwing on the lingerie and breaking out whatever toy you two want to play with and explore whatever ... that is none of my business; but, you don't do that when you aren't being treated like butter.

Think of it this way: you have a lady center which makes you the CEO of the company. You are in charge of what goes down; you run the damn place. Men want what you have, they want the job. Would you give someone a job who wasn't qualified and would hurt your company? Hell to the NO! Do you pay your employees before they do the work or after? If they do the work, and show they are really good at their jobs, you compensate them, and maybe reward them with a bonus if they've gone above and beyond. If they are bad at their jobs you fire them and don't let them keep drawing a paycheck for not living up to their end of the deal. Do you see the parallel in dating? You're the CEO. Don't forget it.

HUNGRY LIKE THE WOLF

Do you know her? The one who is hungry like the wolf and on the hunt? If you are friends with her, you owe it to all of womanhood to stop her in her tracks. If she is willing to sleep with strange men on first dates or someone's husband, what do you think she would do to you someday if you met a good man? Women who treat dating like a way to fill their lipstick cases with notches are the ones ruining your dating life. Men don't need to make a commitment to you if they can go on an app and have a lonely, horny, girl with low self-esteem fuck them within an hour. These girls are putting prostitutes out of business. I have way more respect for the prostitutes than girls who give away sex for free. At least the prostitute risked her health for money to take care of herself, and got money to pay to go the doctor if she caught something nasty. I know, women can do whatever they want with their bodies and we're not supposed to judge, but when their sexual behavior puts you at risk if you might end up with the same man at some point, you should get to have an opinion. And my opinion is that it's this kind of behavior that keeps women from receiving the respect and treatment we deserve in the dating and relationship experience.

I WANNA HAVE SOME FUN

I know if you're considered a naught girl, you may need love too, but is it worth hurting another woman and her children? I feel like I'm always hard on men for being the cheaters, but women are catching up. If you don't like it when someone cheats on you and you've been hurt by cheating, why the hell would you do it to someone else? Ladies, please be a high value, classy woman and end a relationship before you start a new one. Cheating hurts everyone! And God forbid you are sleeping with a man with little children at home, you really need to evaluate what type of person you are. Why would you ever want to hurt another woman and little children? If all women stopped sleeping with married men, imagine how much better we all would be treated. I know some men lie to get you in bed, but this is why you wait to really get to know who he is and see if he is telling you the truth before your lady center goes near his penis.

ELVIRA

Elvira met her husband while he was still married and she became his mistress. He eventually left his wife for her. Yeah, you know what happens next. After their daughter was born he started up with some girl at work. As you might guess, he got fired from his job because of the mess that comes from fishing off the company pier. Elvira wanted to kick his ass out, but she had just had a baby and she was too overwhelmed to make that kind of decision. He went into a deep depression, so she stayed with him. She had to go out and get a job where she worked ten hours a day with a two-hour commute time on top of it so she could now support the family he had failed. The last time I talked to her she was depressed and miserable, but she said she recognized that she was getting what she deserved because she did this to another woman. I really commended her for accepting the karma that comes from treating other people with disrespect and putting bad energy out into the world.

LIKE A VIRGIN

If your man is like a virgin, being touched for the very first time, you are in a great relationship because your body retains the spiritual energy of those you have sex with! I'm not really saying you need to try to date only virgins. The odds of finding a unicorn like that in this day and age who is age-appropriate for you are nil. But, if you can find someone who hasn't been tainted by lots of partners and lots of failed relationships, you stand a much better chance of having a successful relationship with him.

Every sexual interaction involves the fullest exchange possible of our energy. When you have sex with someone who is not good for you, you expose yourself to their lower vibrations, and this can weigh you down spiritually. Having sex with someone isn't just giving someone access to your body; you are giving them access to your dreams of love, your trust that they won't hurt you, your heart, and, most important, your health. A man who doesn't have a polluted sexual energy will be able to honor all of this and keep it safe. Please go online and read more about this!

ATOMIC DOG

Men may be like the famous atomic dog that chases his tail and gets dizzy, or has to chase a new cat because he feels like that. You may not know what the BBD means because you were married. But, if you're dating you're going to need to know what this is. The Bigger Better Deal (BBD) is the mentality that there is always someone better for us out there. There is always a new cat to chase. You will go on great dates only to find that your great date is still looking for someone else online, and it makes you feel like shit, to say the least; but, Flower, don't take it personally. It shows the character of those looking for the BBD, not your value or desirability! They're not ready for a relationship and want to be alone and free.

You will encounter men after your divorce who will be attractive to you, and easy to hang out with, but they might not be good for you and may run from women they perceive as the dogcatcher (women who want a commitment).

Remember, at the beginning of the relationship everyone seems like the greatest person in the world, but who they really are surfaces in time. Men are on their best behavior at the beginning because they are trying to get you to trust them so you'll have sex with them. If you are smart, you will put them on probation and make them prove themselves.

Bad boys will tell you sweet little lies to make themselves look like the good guy, and some of them are really good at it. This is why you have to go slow and let their words be supported by their actions before you believe them.

THE BELL OF ST. MARK

Valerie's husband cheated on her and she was heartbroken. Years later, when she was beginning to allow herself to trust men again, she fell in love. She told her new boyfriend, Mark, about everything that happened to her in her marriage, so he was well aware of the pain she went through, and that she was ready for love and marriage again.

Mark was older, good-looking, caring, and kind—he was St. Mark to her; he was everything she was looking for. Their chemistry was off the charts and they always had fun times together full of laughs. On their first date, she told him that she only likes to date one person at a time and if he was into dating a ton of women she didn't want to see him again. Smart girl! He told her he didn't need to see anyone else and that he wanted to see where it could go. They were like little kids in love, spending as much time together as they could with demanding jobs. Through the course of their relationship she told him exactly what she wanted and needed. He never offered anything specifically one way or another, but acted like he was on board—that they were on their way to getting married and growing old together. He told her he loved her and brought her to his brother's wedding with his older children.

She did think that it was odd that he never wanted to spend time with her kids or with her friends or family, but she rationalized it by telling herself that since they hardly had any free time, he wanted to just be alone with her. Plus, her kids were younger and she didn't want them getting attached to any man until they were ready for engagement.

After a year and a half of dating, she found out he was seeing someone else, and cheated on her many times while they were dating. They took a little break at one point, but he sent her gifts and tried to get back together with her. She decided not to confront him about what he was doing and to take a different approach. She told him in a kind, loving way that she wasn't going to have sex with him again until they were engaged because she was starting to feel used. He was shocked and proceeded to tell her that he didn't want to get married because if he got divorced again it would be too much paperwork. FYI, they just divided things and didn't even go to court. Clearly, he never intended to give her that kind of commitment and was hoping he could string her along for the sex for as long as possible. If the Bell of St. Mark was really a saint, it was at the *church of a poison mind*. He wasted a year and a half of her life so he could get laid and have some companionship ... not very saintly behavior.

The last time she saw him, he told her he loved her and that he would call her the next day but never did. I guess when he found out the free sex was over, he decided to bail. Six months later, on Christmas day, she got a text with a bunch of stupid emojis wishing her a Merry Christmas like nothing had happened. My guess is he was probably lonely and wanted to get the sex back. She obviously didn't respond. Smart Flower!

I can give you so many stories about selfish men like this who strung a woman along that would make you sick. They only care about themselves and don't care if you are upset when they break up with you; they got what they wanted. This is an example of how important it is, if you want to get married, to make sure you hear him say he wants it too! Those words didn't come out of this man's mouth because he knew if he told Valerie he didn't want to get married, she wouldn't have dated him and he wouldn't have gotten the sex from her!

I did ask Valerie what her part was in the failure of this relationship, she told me her intuition was off the charts telling her something was wrong and she was in the *danger zone*. She was also drinking too much because he liked to drink. Every time she felt weird about something she would talk to him about it and he would have a great explanation and excuse and he would calm her fears temporarily. Sometimes he even made her feel bad for questioning him. (Flowers, this is known as *gaslighting*.) He even managed to force a few tears over how it made him feel that she would think he could be a bad guy—that she would ever think that he would do bad things. She wanted to believe his lies because she loved him and he said was telling her he loved her too. She let that hope drown out what she knew, when her intuition was clearly saying he was not an honorable man and didn't care about her.

This is why the smartest thing a woman can do when

dating these days is to wait until he is fully committed before she gives him her body and risks an STD. One out four people have one. Can you imagine if all women got together, stopped sleeping with married men, and didn't have sex without an engagement ring what would happen? We would all have very big shiny rings and wouldn't get fucked over and cry over men who aren't honorable. This is why the smartest thing a woman can do dating in this day and age is to reserve that part of yourself that is most vulnerable and deserves the most love and care. And Flowers, like I've said before, I'm not a prude at all. I'm all for the sex - a lot of the sex and trying new exciting things to keep the sex alive, but that reward is giving to a man when you have a solid commitment and you can trust him. But, all hope is not lost.

I can't talk about a man that selfish and awful, and not give you an example of the type of guy that you are going to end up with if you make the right choices in dating. In fact, I'm going to give two examples because love exists and good men are out there. I'm a hopeless romantic and believe in love. There are loving and kind men out there who would never hurt a woman or disrespect them in any way. So, here is proof for all of you who are getting leery out there in the dating world.

TOM SAWYER

Tom Sawyer met Sara online, and he knew she was the one pretty quickly. On the second date he asked her all the hard relationship questions so he didn't waste his time with a girl who was just out for something to do until she met someone else. He was really excited to meet her children and then loved spending time with them. Tom was divorced and had older children in college, while Sara had little kids were young. He was very accepting of her young children, which is rare in dating today. Most men run from women with small kids, and don't want the financial responsibility.

He treated her and her children with such love and respect. He always surprised her with little thoughtful gifts, planned great thoughtful dates, and was always there for her when she needed him. This is what a man looks like, someone who will be a good husband.

Yup, they got married and are living the great second marriage dream full of happiness. Yes, she still has to deal with an ex-husband because she has little kids, but her new husband has been so respectful toward her ex, which allows the marriage to have way fewer complications. And let me tell you her ex is a jerk, so her new husband is a really good man. Sara had high standards, and Tom Sawyer was ready and willing to meet them.

Darling Flower, Tom Sawyer is the good guy, the guy you want—the guy you will find when you keep your standards very high. It might take a while to find him, but it's better to wait for him than to waste your time on a guy like The Bell of St. Mark.

JOHNNIE B GOOD

Johnnie dated Jamie for about four months, and then they both agreed they weren't right for each other. Also, Johnnie was moving out of state. Two years later he was planning to visit Jamie's town and asked Jamie if she would like to go out to dinner. Jamie really didn't want to go but forced herself because she really needed to get out of the house and do something. Jamie was fifty-eight and had given up on dating and finding the right guy. She was a writer and had another part time job that she really didn't like but needed to pay the bills.

Well, on that date something shifted. Johnnie and Jamie realized that they were right for each other. Long story short, only a few months later Johnnie asked Jamie to marry him and move to be with him. Moving wasn't a big sacrifice for her because of the work she did, and in moving she would be able to drop the part-time job. He wanted her to focus on her writing. High standards and waiting for the right guy got her the guy and the career she wanted. When I spoke to her she was glowing, and she said she felt like she was in a dream, so I pinched her!

Darling Flower, your guy is out there, and sometimes he comes later on in life. A man like this is worth the wait. Your second husband needs to be all that and a bag of chips. This guy was the family size bag of chips, that came with free soda and chocolate. You don't want to get divorced again or be unhappy because you were lonely and settled for someone. Wait for him, and work on you!

PHOTOGRAPH

He's got a photograph, a picture of ... something that should be private. Some of you will be thinking, *I would never do this,* but some of you will be thinking that it's okay and fun to send men naked photos that are *for your eyes only* and I'm just being a prude. Those naked photos of you can and will be used in court against you if you are going through a divorce or, God forbid, a custody battle. I know it's fun sending a little sexy pic to remind a man that you're a beautiful sexy Flower, but not while you are going through a divorce. And if you're dating, I would wait until you're married before the naked ones come out. Don't be stupid and think you're the only one sending him free porn. Other women are doing it too if you just started dating or don't have a commitment. Can you imagine if those photos were leaked out? What happens if you find out after a few months of dating that he's cray-cray and puts those photos online, or sends them to your ex. Is this something you would want your kids to see?

Bottom line: If it's a photo you wouldn't feel comfortable putting on social media, you shouldn't send it! Stick to sending sexy tasteful shots, at least in lingerie, and only after several months of dating. Be different; be the girl he wants to marry, not jerk off to. He will always have this photo of you to jerk off to and he may show his friends. I've seen tons of naked women who would be mortified knowing I saw their photo or little strip videos. I'm sure you have guy friends who will attest to the fact that they have tons of naked pics on their phone from women. When you're dating a guy, he probably won't show his friends if he's a good guy; but, years later, after you break up, he may show his friends. *Remember Paula with the big breasts who used to send me pics of her breasts on Tuesdays? Do you remember Brenda's tight butt that you can bounce a quarter off of?* All of my guy friends have tons of naked pictures. My best straight guy friend has a whole library collection, and he's actually one of the good guys. Be classy and different.

I actually walked up to different men every day for one week (who didn't have wedding rings on) and I told them I was writing a book about divorce and dating. I asked them if women send them naked photos and how many they had. Every single one of them had photos, some even showed me! Only one didn't have a fully naked pic, the rest all had a whole collection to spank the monkey to if needed. Your fiancée should have photos of you and your husband, not a man who didn't put a ring on it.

MEETING IN THE LADIES ROOM

You have to look good when you step on the floor! If you are not in a good place emotionally and turn your back for a minute, some other woman will be rocking your man. Hang out with your friends, drink more wine, get more hobbies, but don't date if you:

1. still have trust issues,
2. are angry at your ex,
3. are depressed,
4. have friends and family pressuring you to date

again,
5. are lonely,
6. are bored,
7. miss your ex,
8. are dealing with an ex who has a hot new lady (or an ugly one),
9. have unrealistic expectations of men,
10. don't really love yourself.

MY PREROGATIVE

Of course, you can do what you want to do, but remember you just lost a lot from your first divorce, and I'm sorry to tell you, it can happen again too. So, be super careful out there, protect yourself. Pick the right man this time. There will always be problems in your life, with or without a man, but with a man comes more problems because you are interacting with another human being who's just as flawed as you are. And if you don't have time for all that, stay alone and be happy. Only you know what is best for you. Just don't ever lie and use people to serve your own needs while you're dating. Be honest with men if you're not into them, and treat them with love and respect. If you treat people the way you would like to be treated, you will be able to sleep at night knowing you're a good person who cares about others besides yourself. Yes, you have to put you first, but you can do it truthfully, not hurting anyone or leading them on. I know this seems so logical, but some women have turned into man-eaters, especially after they've been hurt.

MAN-EATER

Whoa, here she comes, and she is ready to chew someone up. Some women adopt personas as they start dating that are unrecognizable based on who they were as a wife and mother. They might target men who are significantly older, or they might go after the boy toy. Sometimes it's true that May-

December romances work. You can't help who you fall in love with, and sometimes that person isn't in your generation. But, most of the time, if you are severely mismatched in age, it also means you aren't on the same page regarding your life path, priorities, life experience, or interests. Flower, don't embarrass yourself by turning into a cougar—or a puma or a jaguar or whatever fits your age range. I know you've heard of Cougars, but did you know there is actually a full Feline Scale to categorize women on the "prowl"? Kind of disgusting, isn't it? Do you want to be a joke? Well, that's part of the dating world now. Are you ready for it?

AT THIS MOMENT

What did you think you would do at that moment when you experienced your first break up after your divorce? When you learn that someone don't love you no more, or if you're still going through your divorce and want to get back together with your husband and he doesn't want to, it's one of the hardest things you can go through. If you are in this place right now, I'm so sorry! It absolutely sucks, and there really isn't anything anyone can do or say to make it better. The only thing that helps is good old time. Well, as we covered in the previous chapters, friends and mixed drinks do help soothe things a bit.

Now that I've offered you a soft shoulder to cry on, I'm going to slap you a little right now because I'm not letting you believe the excuses men tell you when they break up with you, especially after you just went through a divorce. I want your BS translator working at 100 percent, or you shouldn't be dating.

I've talked with hundreds of women about their breakups, and a common thread is that they all think their situation is unique and different and that their guy is unique and different. They really want to believe his excuse because he is different and his excuse is real—he is busy with grad school, work is crazy right now, he isn't financially ready for a relationship, the distance is too hard, he needs some time alone, etc. Men work through these issues all the time with a woman they love, but your guy is using that as his excuse; so, why is that?

Darling Flowers, if he tells you, *I just don't want to be with you,* that will always be the truth, but it's just not politically correct to say that. I know it's painful and hard to hear that he doesn't want to be with you. If you need to believe his excuse to cope after a breakup go ahead and do it, but when you get out of denial you will have to face the fact that he didn't want to be with you and he would be with you if he loved you. No excuse would be necessary. He doesn't feel what you do and it hurts.

I know some beautiful, smart women who believe stupid cliché excuses when they could feel liberated and just tell everyone he broke up with me, he didn't like me, he didn't want to be with me, I wasn't the one, or he wasn't feeling it for me anymore. It actually feels freeing and powerful! But the truth of the matter is so hard for some women to face. When we like someone, we want them to like us back the same way. It's a funny thing that we can see it crystal clear when it's someone else's breakup, but when it's yours it's all foggy.

So, here is your homework: ask five of your male friends what excuse they gave a woman they broke up with; it will help you open your eyes if you're believing excuses. Ask them if the reason they gave was the real reason, and then ask them if they would've broken up with her if they really wanted to be with her. This assignment can help give you some clarity to let go of that relationship and move forward dating a man who isn't too busy with work, too busy with his kids, too busy in grad school, etc. And while you're at it, ask yourself and some girlfriends if you told men straight out that you didn't like them anymore when you broke up with them? Or, did you give them an excuse to soften the blow or to avoid further conflict?

Second assignment: If you want to really dig deep and go through a huge growth spurt in your life, ask yourself why you're having trouble facing the fact that your boyfriend or husband doesn't want to be with you? What does that mean to you? Why is that difficult for you to accept? And if you are clinging to hope, why would you want to be with someone who doesn't want to be with you? Maybe you don't want someone who would kiss the ground that you walk on, or would take twenty years off of his life, because that is a little stalker-ish, but I'm sure you want someone at this moment who wants to hold you again.

HARD TO SAY I'M SORRY
I just want you to know, I really am so sorry if you're hurting. I've been there; we all have. I'm being very direct, telling you what's painfully obvious to everyone but you because I hate when people sugarcoat things and don't say things directly. Some need to hear something hopeful to get through transition, and I provide that for people when necessary, but I know I'm not helping them. I want to see you happy and in love with the right man and never get divorced again. Some breakups and divorces lead to huge emotional and spiritual growth in your life, and it can actually be the best thing that ever happened to you. You probably can't see it now because it hurts, but down the road you will. I know that feels like hollow consolation, but hang in there and you'll see it gets better.

IT'S SO EASY
Dating really is so easy, even though I've given you plenty of warnings about how scary and difficult it is. If your intuition tells you something isn't right ... DON'T GO ON

ANOTHER DATE WITH HIM! Don't question your intuition, just move on. We always know what's right, but we also have a super power for not listening to ourselves and make fabulous excuses for a man. You're divorced and getting a second chance to do it right, so do it right this time. Establish ground rules for yourself and don't let your head or lady center override them, EVER! You might still be questioning your ability to judge a situation, and if that is the case, don't dive into the dating pool until you can trust yourself. If you can't trust the judgement God gave you to take care of yourself and judge right vs. wrong, you can't date! I didn't make the rule; it is what it is.

WHEN IT'S LOVE
How do you know when it's love? How do you feel when it's love? Nobody can really tell you, but when it's real love it will last forever. This is the most important thing that I'm going to tell you when you start dating again after a divorce, or you are considering working things out with your ex. You never need to spend your precious moments on this earth overthinking or making excuses for a man, ever! You could read relationship books all day and night, you will hear the same thing said over and over in different ways when this is the only thing you need to know:

A MAN IN LOVE WITH YOU WILL FIND A WAY TO BE WITH YOU AND DO ANYTHING AND EVERYTHING TO MAKE IT HAPPEN.

Chapter 9
TELL HER ABOUT IT

As someone who knows the pain of divorce, you really owe it to your fellow ladies and gentleman in relationships to support them and help them avoid going down a potentially dangerous path. Tell them about what you've learned. Help people who are considering marriage, whether you were able to save your marriage or decided divorce was your best option.

Everyone sees the potential problems that may lead a couple to a divorce, and most are afraid to say anything; but you have to. It is your duty as a divorced person to warn others about divorce and the aftermath that comes with it. Would you rather tell him/her now that they're making a mistake, or have to watch them cry going through a divorce?

If they don't plan on having children, or can't have children, that's the best-case scenario you'll encounter. When children become involved, that ex will be in their life forever and children will be hurt. If you can help them avoid that pain, don't you think you should?

I know you feel bad telling a person you love negative things about love and marriage when they are about to take the big plunge. Honestly, I would question what type of person you are if you didn't feel badly as you tell someone they are about to make the biggest mistake of their life. You're a good person and don't want to hurt your loved one, but staying silent can cause them a lot more pain for a lot longer time. Yes, it will hurt in the moment, but it will be nothing compared to what she will go through if she marries the wrong man.

GOODBYE TO YOU

I CAN'T WAIT

No bride can wait for her wedding day; she loves him even though he doesn't try. She's in her own little world where she thinks their love can't die. She's got a big, shiny engagement ring, and she's not afraid to show it off! Her clock is ticking away, and she's all about having that big beautiful party. She has checked and rechecked her guest list a hundred times and you know she picked out her wedding dress years ago. She's already asked all of her friends to be bridesmaids, and they've all been out shopping and drinking, trying to find the perfect dress they all can agree upon. She's already decided she's going to have three kids—Heather, Axl, and Slash—by natural birth, and they will buy a home in Westchester, NY. It's all planned out and her dream is coming true, this is what she has been waiting for.

The groom is only thinking about the honeymoon with his perfect bride, and the occasional annoyance of having to pick between Candlelight and Swiss Coffee, which both look like the same white to him. But, he's madly in love and wants to give her anything she wants so he pretends to be interested in flower arrangements and place cards and registering for things he can't imagine they'll ever use. He's just looking forward to all the sex (and those things she won't do now because he's gotta put a ring on it first) he believes he's going to get every day when he gets married. He thinks she's going to cook dinner every night and do his laundry (while naked). He's still going to go out with his friends all the time and do all the same fun guy things he used to do before he got married.

Yeah, someone needs to give both of them a reality check.

DON'T DREAM IT'S OVER

Hey now, hey now, believe me, most women have that little intuitive voice in their hearts telling them when it's not a good idea to get married and to cancel the wedding, but she can't do it because she really wants to get married. She's been waiting for this day since she was a little girl and doesn't want to give up on her dream. It may not be the guy she is in love with so much as it is the dream of being married . . . or maybe just having the dream wedding. And if it's not about that, then it might be the dream of what she believes he can be, not who he currently is.

Men don't want to be embarrassed and cancel the wedding. He doesn't want to tell people that his fiancée is sleeping with the janitor at his office that she met when she stopped by to take him to lunch one day. He has the need to win her love and protect his ego. Maybe, he thinks she won't do it when they get married? Who knows? Love makes people rationalize things we would tell our friends not to tolerate.

She can be the biggest bitch on the planet, but he will still think she is not sleeping with Prince and the whole Revolution. Most men think women don't cheat and lie as much as they do, but statistics are showing that the ladies are catching up, and men aren't as strong as us in handling the pain of infidelity.

BURNING DOWN THE HOUSE

Hold Tight! You might be in for some nasty weather. If you see someone you love heading into a marriage that is headed for disaster and you don't say anything. We all want to enjoy our lives to the fullest like everyone claims on their dating profiles, but if you have to be around people you don't like, your life may suck. If your son or daughter is marrying someone you think is going to hurt them, as a parent you have a duty to speak up. Do you really want to have to pretend to like their spouse for however long the marriage lasts? And if they have kids, are you really going to be able to share the holidays and family time with people who are making your loved ones unhappy? You're the parent; do you want to be a part-time grandma/pa, and have other step-grandparents coming in and taking the limited time that you're going to get with your grandchildren after a divorce. I think not.

If you're a true the friend, don't you think you need to say something before you do you want to have to hang out with your friend and this man who is hurting her for the rest of your life? You may not have a friend anymore because you can't deal with the jerk they married. And most woman who marry someone cray-cray stick up for the cray-cray person until they really hurt them or abuse them. Losing friends hurts more than losing a guy sometimes. You might be afraid your friend will choose them over you, and that is possible; but, if you don't tell them how you feel, you could still lose them because you can't sit by and watch them do this to themselves, or they might keep dragging you into the middle of their drama.

If you're the sister/brother do you want this person opening presents with you on Christmas, eating turkey on Thanksgiving? It's okay to be selfish if you're helping save someone from a bad divorce, and making your limited time on the earth more enjoyable. The person your family member or friend marries doesn't have to be someone that you love, but they should be someone who loves your friend well, who is a moral stand up person, and who will be good and faithful to her.

ONCE, TWICE, THREE TIMES A LADY
Are you divorced once, twice, or did you divorce three times, lady? It doesn't really get all that much easier, you just know how to do it now. Men and women really need to be educated about the reality of what life will be like in marriage, and the horrific consequences that may await them if the marriage doesn't work out. The money and the emotional fallout can be devastating. It's so important to choose the right partner,

and wait to get married a bit later in life so you more fully know yourself and know what BS you can handle and what BS you can't, as well as what you really want from a relationship. Marriage is pretty much a 50/50 shot. The real question that people need to ask themselves before getting married, if they want children, is this:

Would I feel safe leaving my child with this man and his family every other weekend?

If the answer is NO, you shouldn't marry him and definitely not have children with him.

You should also find out what type of women he dated before you because some girl is going to be spending time with your future children after you divorce. You can't take a 50/50 chance that your precious child will be left alone with people who are not good and decent salt-of-the-earth people. What if someone you didn't like told you have a 50/50 chance that you will have to give them half your money in about ten years? Or what if you are planning to build a house on land that may not be stable, and it has 50/50 chance that it will fall into the ocean in the next ten years. Would you take the risk with your money or home?

TALK TO ME

I hope before they get married they set their secrets free. In the United States there are two divorces every minute. That's a lot of broken dreams and a hell of a lot of wasted wedding dresses! Every human being should know the statistics on divorce before getting married and should be able to talk to their friends and family what they have done to prepare for their marriage so theirs will survive. It should become common practice for parents and extended family on both sides to sit the engaged couple down and go through marital guidance information. They should have a big dinner where the engaged couple stands up announces their engagement and explains why they believe their marriage will last.

I think it's crazy that our culture doesn't encourage more community involvement in this process. I know you're probably thinking that is way too intrusive and it's the couple's decision alone. But, think about it; who has to come in and help the broken family with raising the children, covering the financial strain of two households, and deal with all of the emotional fallout when they end up divorced? The friends and family, that's who! So, they should get to weigh in and express their opinions.

ONE IN A MILLION
Are you the one and second to none? Well, you have a shot at it at least. We commonly quote the statistic that 50 percent of first marriages end in divorce, but that number includes marriages that end in legal separation as well. Here is a breakdown?

- 20% end within 5 years
- 32% end within 10 years
- 40% end within 15 years
- 48% end within 20 years

What about your second marriages? Second marriages have a much lower success rate than first marriages. You would think some first marriage practice would increase the odds for success, but it doesn't.

- 10% end within 1 year
- 31% end within 5 years
- 46% end within 10 years

Now, what about third marriages? They seriously should work out since the third time is the charm, right? Wrong!

Oy Vey, the divorce rate for a third marriage is 73%. Things actually get worse statistically when it comes to marriages. Three out of four third marriages will end up in divorce. You would think people are getting too old and too tired to go through a third divorce.

IN MY HOUSE

Welcome to my house, you can move right in without a commitment and it's going to work out like butter! Another misconception is that you would have a better chance for marriage when you test out the waters, but that isn't true either! People tend to think that living with someone before marriage will increase the odds of divorce, but recent divorce statistics show that living with someone doesn't affect whether your marriage will fail or have success.

- 29% of marriages that begin without cohabitation fail within 10 years
- 33% of marriages that begin with cohabitation and engagement fail within 10 years
- 39% of marriages that begin with cohabitation but without engagement fail within ten years

HOT FOR TEACHER

So what two things help a little beating out the divorce statistics? A college education and age! So let that teacher teach you all you need to know and don't get married too early.

1. People who attend college marry later in life and tend to make more money than those who don't attend college, which increase the odds of marital success.

- Less than High School - Women: 39%, Men: 54%
- High School - Women: 41%, Men: 47%
- Some College - Women: 49%, Men: 54%
- Bachelor's Degree - Women: 78%, Men: 65 %

2. As it turns out, age plays a big role in determining a marital success. People who marry under the age of 20 have the highest rate of divorce—they are 1.5 times as likely to get divorced as those who get married between the ages of 20 to 24 years old. Those who marry after the age of 25 are even

less likely to get divorced.

TRUE BLUE

I'm sure you've had a lot of guys in your life, looked into their eyes and wondered whether you will stay together. Curious about whether where you live makes a difference? Do red states have less divorce than blue ones?

What are the top states for divorce? Please not that some states don't track their divorce rate. California, Georgia, Hawaii, Indiana, Louisiana, and Minnesota don't track divorce rates, but of the others, these are the top states for divorce:

- 1st: Nevada - 5.6
- 2nd: Arkansas - 5.3
- Tied for 3rd, 4th: Oklahoma and West Virginia - 5.2
- 5th: Idaho - 4.9
- Tied for 6th, 7th: Alaska and Wyoming - 4.8
- 8th: Florida - 4.5
- Tied for 9th, 10th: Colorado and Kentucky - 4.4

So, basically if you live in Nevada, are under the age of twenty-five, and didn't go to college, *WTF are you thinking?* It would be crazy to thinking getting married! Although, I guess it's a little fitting that so many people go to Vegas for quickie, impulse marriages. Please don't have children until your marriage proves me wrong after ten years.[7]

SAY IT ISN'T SO

You know you want to say it isn't so. But if it is so and a person close to you is marrying someone whose fiancée has any of these issues, you really must sit them down and have a heart-to-heart and do your best to help them avoid a tragedy. Does their significant other:

- have any type of alcohol, drug, gambling, or sex

---

7   https://www.avvo.com/legal-guides/ugc/marriage-divorce-statistics

addiction;
- hide texts, emails, and phone calls from them;
- act in a controlling manner or try to change things that don't need changing;
- have a shitty family that everyone hates;
- have a shitty family that has and created they have severe emotional or mental issues because of them;
- have different religious or spiritual beliefs that they can't reconcile;
- act like a toddler when they don't get their way;
- pick at your loved one and put them down;
- have serious financial problems or an unhealthy relationship with money;
- have lots of critics and tend to rub everyone the wrong way?

If anyone thinks they are going to beat out the 50/50 divorce rate when any of the above are present, they really need to wake up and do some soul searching! I know we are all a bit dysfunctional in our own way, but having complex more issues can almost guarantee a divorce.

WHAT YOU DON'T KNOW
Some people tend to take the "ignorance is bliss" attitude and believe that what you don't know won't hurt you. People tend to have different feeling on this subject. Some people think what you don't know might hurt you, or what you don't know won't hurt you. We all have different opinions. But, I'd like you to consider, if you were about to make a life-long commitment to another human being, would you want to know before you got married that they were cheating and lying, or a shitty person in general? If you could go back in time and listen to your intuition (or the people who that warned you, or actually get a warning from the people who were too afraid to tell you) would you want the information?

Most people would say yes. I know that I wish I'd had that information. Several of my ex's friends knew he was cheating on me while we were dating with our mutual friend Carrie. I wouldn't have married him if I had known, and that information would've saved me a lot of pain. And it would've saved my ex a lot of money in the divorces that he fought to pay all these years. When he's mad about giving me money to help support our kids, I wonder if he thinks, *If I had just told her the truth about cheating then I wouldn't have to give her any money and she could've been with a good man.* Yeah, I bet that's not what he is thinking! I often wonder what my life would have been like if one person had had the balls to tell me about what he was doing, or if he had come clean with me before I married him the first time. Obviously, I'll never know, but I will always wonder.

I'M ON FIRE

Tell me, is he good to you? That's not a question we ask as often as we should, yet we don't seem to have trouble asking people about other aspects of life. People tell their family members all the time to exercise to prevent heart disease. They advise you not to eat too much sugar to prevent diabetes and cancer. Watch your diet so you don't get fat. They caution you to slow down when you're driving so you don't get into an accident. They tell you to watch that investment and; sell that stock before it depreciates. We watch out for each other in a lot of ways, because it's the right thing to do. We also offer a lot of unsolicited advice and aren't afraid to offer our two cents on a whole lot of topics; but, for some reason, we don't feel that it's as important to watch out for someone who is getting into a risky relationship. Their lady center or penis won't literally be on fire, but if they get an STD it will sure feel like it.

I wholeheartedly believe you need to tell someone when his or her significant other is cheating. A person's health is being endangered. If someone needs CPR, you wouldn't hesitate to give it to him or her. You wouldn't sit there and let them die! The Good Samaritan law (that protects you if you accidentally hurt someone while trying to save their life) should be in effect for affairs as well! You could save a person from HPV, HIV, Hepatitis, etc. You have to tell your friends and family when their health is being endangered! I don't understand why people don't look at this as a medical/ health issues as opposed to simply an emotional issue. Yes, it will hurt their heart, but it can also harm their body.

SPIES LIKE US
Remember, love is deaf, dumb, and blind. If you are really certain someone is cheating on your loved one, you have to go in with some proof. You'd better have names, dates, and pictures. Nobody wants to receive the information you are about to present, so they are likely to refuse to listen if you don't have anything to support your claims. You might want to act like a P.I. yourself, but be careful. People who are behaving immorally and don't want to get caught can do some crazy things to avoid getting busted. You might want to hire a professional instead to dig up the dirt you need. PI's will tell you there is nobody who spies like us. They know all the tricks of the trade and can get you the info you need without putting yourself in potential danger and wasting a lot of your time. Sometimes it's worth throwing money at problems and sometimes it's not. In this case, it's worth it to save the amount of money and pain from the aftermath of a bad divorce.

OPEN ARMS
Before you tell someone that their fiancée is opening their arms or anything else to another man or woman, make sure they are not in an open relationship. I would ask that question first before you bring up cheating. Nowadays open

relationships are working for some and are considered to be very acceptable. There are men and women who love dating people in open relationships because they don't have to deal with the complications of a relationship and get sex without paying for it or having to give a commitment. I would never consider it in a million years for myself, but it works for some and I'm not here to judge what's right for another human being. But, my point is, you will look stupid if you tell him that his fiancée is sleeping with the buff check out boy at the grocery store when that's part of their arrangement.

WHITE WEDDING

Hey little Flower, what have you done? If you have been asking this of your friend or family member and they are still going ahead with the marriage, you should seriously consider whether you should go to a wedding to support a relationship that you know in your heart will not work out. They're young, he already cheated on her, he doesn't have a job, she's in denial, and you have to give a gift and drive or fly and out of town and get a hotel room to attend a wedding you don't agree with. I don't think so. Would you go to the funeral of someone you hate? Not likely. I think it's disingenuous to show up for something you don't support.

When you believe someone is making a mistake, speak up, and then stick to your guns by not attending the party for doomed relationship.

LAY IT DOWN

How do you do it? How do you lay down the truth to your friend? You say a quick prayer, take a deep breath, and give it to them lovingly, sweetly, directly, and thoroughly. Think of what would be best for your friend. I've had several people I've had to tell that someone was cheating on them. One person I told was in deep denial, and she needed the intervention with proof. A lot of proof. As much proof as we gave her, it never seemed to be enough. Please think of your friend and what would be best for them, not for you. Denial can be really hard to penetrate.

TAKE ON ME

What is your take on how they will act to the news? You should be prepared for all the possible outcomes.

1. Are they your bat shit crazy friend we all know and love? Consider taking back up if they might overreact.
2. Are they on the 3:00 denial train headed to nowhere? You might need to be equipped with proof.
3. Do they know their significant other has been hanging out with other penises or lady centers, or both? Maybe you should get them some antibiotics.
4. Are they the type to blame everyone else? It could be a good idea to wear armor.
5. Do they make excuse after excuse for their fiancée? Be prepared to say what you have to say and walk away.
6. What kind of advice have they offered in the past? You might want to use some of their own words on them.
7. How did they handle conflict with you or others? Again, you might want to keep that armor with you.
8. Are they religious? Do they believe in forgiveness? Hopefully they will forgive you for delivering the bad news.
9. Are they Italian with a temper? Maybe you should you hide the knives.
10. Are they really fragile? Maybe it's a good idea to hide all pain killers, carpet cleaner, and alcohol first.

I'M STILL STANDING

You might still be standing after telling your friend their

love is cheating or is a bad person in another way, but your relationship with them may not be. Killing the messenger is a saying for a reason. When we hear distressing news it activates our fight or flight response and lash out at something; but, as is often the case, it's the wrong thing because the person in the wrong isn't there when they get the news. This is the number one reason people don't want to speak up and tell their loved one that someone is cheating or not marriage material.

Throughout history the messenger has been blamed for the distressing news and takes the hit for it. In Anthony and Cleopatra, Shakespeare writes that Cleopatra threatens to treat the messenger's eyes as balls, when she learns that Anthony has married another woman. It's never a fun position to be in when you have to deliver bad news. Just remember that whatever blowback you experience is not about you at all and that when the dust settles you'll be able to live with yourself, knowing you did the right thing.

ANGELINE

Angeline was very religious and married her husband when she was only eighteen years old. Her husband was a recovering alcoholic who turned to God instead of AA. He already had a few kids from some of his previous wives. She raised one of his sons from the time he was a little boy because his mom abandoned him, and then they had one daughter together. Twenty years later, he started an affair with his son's mom. She was always the love of his life, but she was very dysfunctional and couldn't provide a family structure. Angeline knew what was going on with them because she saw her husband's phone call list and emails, but she wasn't able to admit it to herself. She was in full-blown denial. Even when another family member called and confirmed the affair, she didn't want to believe her. She told herself that she was just being vindictive because she was divorcing out of the family. This is the power of denial. Your intuition can know what is true, you can have proof right in front of you via email and phone records, and you can even have someone tell you, but you still won't accept the truth. No one wants to believe that the person they love would betray them. It can take a long time to come to terms with what is right in front of someone when them are in denial, and there is nothing you can do to make them face the facts. You just have to be willing to be there for them when reality comes crashing down on top of them.

YOU GIVE LOVE A BAD NAME

There is a right way and a wrong way to tell someone their fiancé or spouse is giving love a bad name. It starts with being really loving and kind. Remember, they're about to get shot through the heart, so proceed with caution. Here are your options:

1. Don't tell them at all! Go to the disloyal ass who's cheating and tell them that you know and you're going to tell your friend on Saturday at 6:00 p.m. if they don't come clean on their own. If they deny it, which they will, tell them you have proof. I highly recommend using your phone to record the conversation in case you need it. Let the cheating fiancé do it so you don't have to get in the middle and risk getting in trouble with your friend. If he tells her that you made them do it, admit to it. Say, "Yes, I did give him the ultimatum. I thought he should do it, not me. I love you and I care about your health and I couldn't stand by watching you marry a cheater."

2. Anonymously send them a letter. I actually know several women who did it this way. Hopefully, you have a picture or a name of the other party to send with it. If you can, contact the person they're

cheating with and get some info that could help your cause. Maybe, they don't even know the person is in a committed relationship, let alone getting married. It helps to have it all in writing. Be careful with this though; personally, if I found out a friend sent me this letter instead of telling me face to face, I would be mad. But, I'm the type of person who wouldn't hold it against them and would be thankful. Not all women would act the same. You usually know how your friends will respond to the news.

3. Hire a P.I. If you have money, you should hire a private investigator to help out with the situation. Only do this if you are sure and you know your friend/family member will be in denial without substantial proof. You could stake them out with a mutual friend and get the proof yourself, if you can't afford to hire someone. It could take weeks of sitting and waiting, but would be well worth it if you get what you need and save ya a ton of money.

4. Do it in private. If you don't want to get all of your other friends involved because you think it would embarrass them more, then tell them by yourself. If you're her BFF, you have to. Be prepared for her to accuse you of being jealous of her marriage. She is likely to turn it around on you, so make sure you have more than words to back up your accusations. There is so much comfort in denial; nobody wants to believe this is happening to them. Be so sensitive about it. You've probably been cheated on yourself because many people cheat, so you know how much this news will hurt.

5. Hold an intervention. Call all the friends and family and have a big Come to Jesus Meeting with her. Point out all of his flaws while drinking iced tea! Alcohol is not to be involved. Take time and care to make

your case and be loving and gentle along the way. You know you're going to encounter some resistance, so just go slowly and give them time for it to sink in. Make sure they know this is done out of love and that you will be there for support through it all.

Remember, the news of infidelity is traumatic, and trauma causes severe pain. One of the greatest tragedies of relationships is that when people experience the kind of severe pain that comes from a broken heart, they can become suicidal. This is a very delicate matter and it's not funny at all. More women are cheating these days and men have a higher suicide rate than women after a divorce. Men don't have the same support systems or feel the freedom to talk about their feelings the way women do. Especially if they were blindsided by the news that the relationship/marriage was having issues, it can be really hard to cope.

I read a study from the National Institute for Healthcare Research in Rockville, MD that indicated that divorced people are three times as likely to kill themselves as people who are married. The Institute indicates that divorce ranks as the number-one factor in suicide rates in major U.S. cities. I don't share this to discourage you from telling someone what they need to know, but to make you aware of how delicate this information can be and to use the utmost care when sharing it. Also, please make sure you stay connected with your loved one, even if they try to push you away, so you can make sure they are getting the help they need to deal with the fallout of what has happened.

GARY

This was the worst story that I've ever been told. Gary was the good guy all women say they want, but they usually find him to be a bit boring and too nice, even though he was tall, good-looking, and made a nice middle-class income.

Jenny knew Gary was one of the good guys, and she cared about him. She knew he wouldn't cheat on her and would be a good father and a good husband. She was sick of dating and her baby making clock was ticking away, so she married him. They had two beautiful children together, lived in a nice house, and she only worked a part-time job so she would have time for her husband and children and the things she wanted to do. Unfortunately, she met another man at work, and left her husband.

Long story short, he was devastated over the divorce. Jenny got married right away and moved in with the man she was cheating on him with and, all of a sudden, he had to share his children with another man. He couldn't handle the pain and killed himself.

Thankfully, this is the only time I've heard of a man taking his life over the pain of infidelity from someone I know, but it does happen more often than we would like to think. Two small children lost their father and Jenny had to live with the fact that she was the reason he killed himself. I know it isn't directly her fault, but if she had kept the vow she made this wouldn't have happened.

Suicide rates are at an all-time high. And when men are going through the turmoil of a horrible unwanted divorce, some of them look to suicide as a way out of the emotional and financial pain. The bitterness and depression and the sense that life isn't worth living anymore without their family can lead to a fatal decision.

Encourage men to seek therapy after a divorce in a light gentle way, especially, if you have a brother or child that is going through a divorce. Please really be there for them! Sometimes the people who need the most help are the ones who say they don't. Be attuned and reach out. That's the best, and sometimes only thing you can do.

SHANDI

Shandi was in the entertainment industry and her husband fucked one of her bridesmaids on her wedding night. Her reception was at a beautiful, expensive hotel, her husband of five hours took his new wife's bridesmaid into her room during the reception and they did the wild thing. She found out when her daughter was five years old and she divorced him. Now, she has to pay him palimony because she makes way more money than he does. How do you like them apples? It took Shandi years to get over the pain that her bridesmaid and husband caused her. She didn't date for a long time because she lost faith in people and her lack of trust stayed with her for a long time. She sunk into a depression and got super thin. Her work also suffered and she lost a job that she needed because of her health problems.

Luckily, most women get therapy immediately when the shit hits the fan or go to their primary doctor and get some antidepressants so they can function and take care of their kids. Females also tend to have good friends they can call at any hour of the night and cry to. We usually have a good mom and family to turn to that will check on us all the time and make sure we are on our way to getting ourselves back together again. Eventually, Shandi looked after herself, but it took time to get back what she lost during that time.

I WANT CANDY

Woman are way less likely to commit suicide after a divorce, but they are more likely to dabble in some candy. I know several women who got addicted to pain killers during their divorce. They had minor surgery and loved the numb feeling that the painkillers gave them to avoid the physical pain from the surgery and the emotional pain from their divorce. This is more common than you think. These women were all women you would never ever imagine would have that type of problem. They were all amazing moms, with good jobs and good families. The pain is real, pretty Flowers, and the pain killer can offer temporary relief; but, the flip side is that it can also cause long-term problems.

Opioid addiction is at an epidemic level here in the US. If you notice a friend using pills to cope with their emotional hardship, consider another type of intervention to help them get the help they need.

ALL I NEED IS A MIRACLE

She's going to stay if she wants to stay, or go if she wants to go. If she hates you right now and the wedding is still on, let's hope you're dead wrong about the person and she has the happiest marriage ever and you have to eat your words. Maybe, that ass she married turns into a good person that treats her with love and respect. God tells us to believe in miracles, and here's where you can put that faith to the test. If she doesn't listen to you, maybe God set this up as a lesson for her learn from.

We all know losing someone you love is deeply painful and teaches us a lot. Personally, I've learned way more from failed relationships than I ever did from the amazing ones. I'm really thankful for all of my relationships because they gave me my greatest life lessons, and I wouldn't be the person I am today without them. Look back at your life too, and think about the times that were rough, how you got through them, and what you learned. Hopefully, this will be a time of growth for her and it's a great thing that she didn't listen to your fabulous advice.

SHE BLINDED ME WITH SCIENCE

So, she's getting blinded with a lot more than science right now. And she can't see, hear, or comprehend what you are trying to get across. And maybe, she is mad or really annoyed that your dropping some purple rain on her parade. At least you said your peace. You don't need everyone to like you; you're not running for mayor. She won't be mad at you later on when she's getting a divorce. She will say she wished she listened to you. You can then say, "I told ya so." Well, maybe you shouldn't say that, but I bet she's going to learn some major life lessons that needed to be learned. You don't know what her path is, and she doesn't know what yours is, so it's best to just worry about your own path most of the time. But, if you can spare someone the journey you've just taken, then why wouldn't you?

SWEET CHILD O' MINE

Could you look into those eyes of the bluest skies and know you might be causing them future pain? This is the most important reason that you tell someone that their spouse is cheating or won't make a good husband. Children! When you don't tell your friend or family member about the things their future spouse may be doing to hurt them, their future children are inevitably going to suffer. If you knew someone had a drug/alcohol problem wouldn't you step in to make sure no child got hurt because of it? I get that people don't want to insert themselves into someone else's relationship troubles, but if you know your friend wants children with someone who isn't going to be a good spouse, then you really have too. Or, at least give them this book and make them read it so they are clear about the difficulties of marriage and how it can hurt children. Then you will have done your part and won't feel guilty later on. Everyone likes to say that children are okay through the divorce, because it makes them feel less guilty for the mistake they made. Some men leave and don't have to see the mess they made, they leave their ex to clean up the mess they made. I see this over and over and it really makes me sick. Having children with the wrong person is the worst possible thing you can do in your life. It's a huge mistake that should be brought up all the time when you are teaching others about relationships. This is a serious matter that should be addressed and openly talked about, so we can stop children's parents from divorcing every two minutes. Yes, it may be too late for you, but if we could all help one child not go through pain, imagine how our world would change. If we teach people to not cheat and wait to get married our world would be a better place. Going to a great college and   getting a good job means shit if you picked the wrong partner to have child with.

You've been through a lot, pretty Flower. Hopefully, you fought for your marriage by making yourself better and trying to get your husband on the same page. If you decided divorce was inevitable, at least you did it with your eyes wide open and were prepared as best you could be for what was to come and made the best choices possible to minimize the damage. And now you have found a new love for your life in yourself, and that is an amazing gift. Now it's your turn to help other women find that gift for themselves by sharing what you've learned in the process and by helping them discover how to love the most important person in their world-themselves.

Conclusion
WHEN ALL IS SAID AND DONE

Thank you for reading my book. I seriously hope you saved your marriage or your divorce is going as smoothly as possible. I hope you are learning everything you can from your transition. If you're not truly sure about leaving your spouse, hang in there and give it all you've got to make it work. Miracles do happen and people fall back in love every day. If you don't fall back in love with your husband and you chose to fall in love again, pick a great loving man with integrity to give your heart to. They are out there.

Only you know what is best for you. I personally support you on whatever decision you make because I know you're a smart Flower. I know you will make the most well-informed decisions that you can. There is a great lesson to be learned in your situation, but please make sure you get yourself in a really healthy place before you make a major, life-changing decision that will affect the rest of your life. Timing is key.

Remember to be careful with who you talk to about your transition. Everyone's transition is different. Some of my friends ended up in new marriages, and some are still single and can't find anyone. Some are happier divorced and some are not. Some got amazing jobs and are doing well financially and some can't pay the bills and struggle. Some of their kids are doing well and thriving and some turned to drugs and have problems in school. You don't know what will happen to you. Life can take you either way.

Please help me spread the word about the dangers of marrying the wrong person. All divorced people must help prevent marriages from failing and teach others about what constitutes a good marriage with the right person. If you do stay with your husband, help others when you know they are having problems. We all need to do our share to save love and marriage, not just for the couple, but for the children suffering the harsh consequences.

Remember, the only person you will have *endless love* with is you. You are the love of your life and have to live with you forever. Open your heart and love another human again if you want too! If you get the chance for a beautiful marriage with a good man, don't be afraid—go for it! Life is short; take the chances you are afraid to take and live a fabulous life. Laugh, smile, dance, and enjoy it, whether you are single, divorced or married.

Much Love, Joy, and Happiness pretty, Flower!
Annette Marie

Beverly Hills Eulogy
THE IMPORTANCE OF A EULOGY

I've talked to hundreds of people in divorce situations and there is a need for closure. That's why it is imperative to have a Eulogy after the loss of a spouse or partner—whether through death, divorce, or major loss of any kind. A Eulogy helps us attain the closure we need to move on with our newly altered life. It helps us make peace with our new existence and ourselves.

Unfortunately, most people will experience the heart-wrenching pain of a breakup at some point in their life. If you've never experienced just how painful a horrific divorce or an unwanted breakup can be, it may be difficult to appreciate how painful it can be. Psychological research shows that divorce and breakups warrant the same emotional response as death or the diagnosis of a life threatening illness. Yet, divorce and breakups are usually treated callously. Often people are not given the time or emotional space needed for bereavement, to mourn the loss of what once was. Unfortunately, "Divorce Eulogies" or simply Eulogies for any kind of emotional closure are not yet enthusiastically accepted. It is time they are!

I really hope that you don't need my service, but if you do, please contact The Beverly Hills Eulogy at thebeverlyhillseulogy@gmail.com. (323) 452-9771

Acknowledgements

To all the beautiful Flowers that found themselves in an Oran "Juice" Jones situation, I'm beyond sorry. I know in time you will be in a loving relationship with an honorable man. This book was written for all of you.

To all the fabulous 80s musicians I've mentioned in my book, you made my life complete and brought me so much joy! The music of the 80s, bottom line is the best music of all time. I have to list my favorite three 80s songs: "November Rain" by Guns N' Roses, "Fascinated" by Company B, and "Total Eclipse" of the Heart by Bonnie Tyler.

My amazing friend Farah, you are the most fabulous Flower in the world. I love you and I will be at your side forever more because that what friends are for. Tony, you, you got what I need, and you are just my best friend. Thanks for always being there for me. Jeff, I'm never gonna eat pancakes again the way I eat pancakes with you you you. My good friend Paul, wait . . . wait, I never had the chance to love you, wait, but it's because you married someone else. Mr. Green, and loving a lighting man isn't always what it's supposed to be, but you know I'm forever yours, Faithfully, Ms. Westwood. To my sister, tell me, Lizzie, do you recognize me? It's been a year, so it doesn't surprise me, last Christmas you didn't come to visit. Deep down you love that song! Dada and Danny, you are the best neighbors and friends that I could ever have. I know in the still of the night my son takes soda and chips from your house. I'm sorry!

Papa can you hear me? Thanks for always being there for me. I love you!

To my cousins Debbie and Victor. You have been together for over twenty years and were blessed with four amazing, smart, and loving children. You have the most beautiful family I've ever seen. Your love for each other is an inspiration to all of us and shows us what marriage is supposed to be like. I grieve with you in the loss of your son Matthew this summer. He was only nineteen years old. No mother should ever have to experience losing a child, and you are an amazing mother who always puts your family first. The pain and loss you are experiencing is unimaginable, and I hope I can be there for you the way you have always been there for me, especially how you help me find my dad who refuses to carry his cell phone.

Made in the USA
Columbia, SC
27 August 2018